Praise for

NEVER HAVE I EVER

"Reading *Never Have I Ever* is a bit like reliving your most awkward moments—but in the best way, because this time, the cringe-worthy moments are happening to someone else. Anyone who's ever swooned over a boy whose name she didn't even know or overanalyzed a text message from a crush will see herself in Katie Heaney. You'll relate to her frustrations and admire her confidence, and probably wish she was your best friend."
—Rachel Bertsche, *New York Times* bestselling author
of *MWF Seeking BFF*

"Katie Heaney is so hilariously fun to read that you may not notice right away how insightful she is about friendship, romance, and the essential weirdness of human relationships."
—Emily Gould, author of *And the Heart Says Whatever*

"Katie's writing is hilarious, and warm, and thoughtful, and reading this book is like having a little version of her to hang out with. What's that, Miniature Paper Katie? You don't like the bath??"
—Edith Zimmerman, founding editor, TheHairpin.com

"Astute and tremendously witty, *Never Have I Ever* chronicles the romantic travails (well, almost romantic) of the very funny Katie Heaney. At some points, I actually got tears in my eyes from laughing too hard."
—Rebecca Harrington, author of *Penelope*

"I challenge any reader to not feel like one of Katie Heaney's closest girlfriends as she examines, in the most charming, honest, original, and amusing way imaginable, how she's managed to never have a date. But don't let the breezy language or topic fool you—this is also a brilliant examination of what it means to be a friend, a girl, and a human being. The first guy to take Heaney out will be very lucky; in the meantime, we her readers are the lucky ones."

—Anna David, *New York Times* bestselling author of *Party Girl* and *Falling for Me*

"No one has ever captured the *angst* and frustration of crushes as perfectly and humorously as Katie Heaney. Anyone who has ever fallen in love with a cute stranger on a train, on the street, in class, or at work will instantly identify with it, and laugh and cringe along with her dating misadventures. But what is most admirable and impressive about this book is how unflinchingly Katie is able to examine herself. As hilariously cutting as she is when describing the male objects of her desire, she's also self-deprecating and introspective. And the book manages to point toward another (oft overlooked) great love in a woman's life: that of her friends."

—Chiara Atik, author of *Modern Dating: A Field Guide*

NEVER HAVE I EVER

My Life (So Far) Without a Date

katie heaney

GRAND CENTRAL
PUBLISHING

NEW YORK   BOSTON

Copyright © 2014 by Katie Heaney

Grand Central Publishing
Hachette Book Group
237 Park Avenue
New York, NY 10017

www.HachetteBookGroup.com

Printed in the United States of America

RRD-C

First Edition: January 2014
10 9 8 7 6 5

Grand Central Publishing is a division of Hachette Book Group, Inc.
The Grand Central Publishing name and logo is a trademark of Hachette Book Group, Inc.

The Hachette Speakers Bureau provides a wide range of authors for speaking events. To find
out more, go to www.hachettespeakersbureau.com or call (866) 376-6591.

The publisher is not responsible for websites (or their content) that are not
owned by the publisher.

Library of Congress Cataloging-in-Publication Data
Heaney, Katie.
    Never have I ever : my life (so far) without a date / Katie Heaney. — First Edition.
        pages cm
    Summary: "I would like to tell you about a theory I've developed about a certain brand of
people I like to call 'lighthouses.' Lighthouse people are beacons that call all the cute sailors
in ships back to land, beckoning them in toward the light. Lighthouse people are magnetic
and luminescent. I am not a lighthouse." So begins Katie Heaney's memoir of her years
spent looking for love, but never quite finding it—from Cody the T-ball player all the way
through college and graduate school heartbreak. By age 25, equipped with a college degree,
a load of friends, and a happy family life, she still has never had a boyfriend...and she's
barely even been on a second date. Throughout this laugh-out-loud funny book, you will
meet Katie's incredible loyal group of girlfriends, including beautiful and fabulous Rylee,
the wild child to Katie's shrinking violet, as well as a whole roster of Katie's crushes. And
you will get to know Katie herself—a smart, modern heroine in the vein of Mindy Kaling
and Sloane Crosley, relaying truths about everything from the subtleties of a Facebook
message exchange to the fact that "Everybody who works in a coffee shop is at least a little
bit hot." Funny, relatable, and inspiring, this is a memoir for anyone who has ever struggled
to find love, but has also had a fair amount of fun in the process"—Provided by publisher.
    ISBN 978-1-4555-4467-7 (pbk.) — ISBN 978-1-4789-5175-9 (audio download) —
ISBN 978-1-4555-4466-0 (ebook)   1. Heaney, Katie.   2. Man-woman relationships—
Humor.   3. Interpersonal relations—Humor.   I. Title.
    HQ801.H425 2014
    302—dc23
                                                                              2013021698

For Rylee, obviously.

Contents

Part Four
GRAD SCHOOL

Introduction
To the Lighthouse

I WOULD LIKE TO TELL YOU about a theory I've developed, in the past two years or so, about a certain brand of people I like to call "lighthouses." This theory was developed after years spent in the company of one such member of the species, carefully observed in her natural habitat. She was the prototype, basically. Her name is Rylee and she's my best friend. You might as well know that now because she's going to come up a lot.

Rylee, since the time I met her seven years ago, has dated nine people. This is probably not remarkably high. It could even be average. What do I know? It could be that that number only seems large in comparison to my own figures, which are so low they're practically negative. But what's really crazy, what's really *impressive* about it, is her lack of time off between boyfriends. When she's single, Rylee hardly needs to leave the apartment (or, in some of those cases, dormitory building) before anywhere from one to four different guys profess an interest in being her next boyfriend. There is a constant stream there. She'll make her interests known, of course, but she always has options. She could sit down on the floor, be still, and wait, and I honestly believe that somebody would show up, sooner or later, to ask her out.

This is what I like to call being "a lighthouse."

Lighthouse people are beacons that call all the sailors in ships back to land, beckoning them in toward the light. Lighthouse people are magnetic and luminescent, so much so that even when one sailor manages to row all the way to land and climbs up into the lighthouse, the rest of the sailors will stay out there on the water, waiting for their chance to come to shore. They will feel that it's always best to keep an eye on the lighthouse, even if they have to come and go due to other sailorly obligations. The lighthouse might act like it doesn't know it's so popular with the sailors, but it does. How could it not? Even if the lighthouse has a special sailor for the moment, its light is always on. It can't help it.

Now, I've had it pointed out to me (by a bunch of boys who couldn't possibly understand the metaphor) that this is not how lighthouses actually "work." These jerks tried to tell me that lighthouses are actually there to keep sailors *away* from particularly dangerous shorelines, because otherwise they'd crash into the jagged rocks found there. I mean, fine. If you want to get technical about certain structures' designated functions, then yes, that is correct, even though I think that's dumb because people and creatures are drawn toward light and if lighthouses really wanted to keep people away from rocky shores they'd be big audio speakers that played scary ghost sounds. But I still think I'm right, in the metaphorical sense. And anyway, this is my book, goddammit. Lighthouses will work the way I want them to. And the lighthouses of my world are big, sexy, maneaters. They don't even try to be that way. They just are.

I am not a lighthouse.

The first time I told Rylee that she was a lighthouse, she asked me what that made me. (Lighthouses generally recognize those that are—and aren't—fellow lighthouses.) I thought about it for a minute. I said: "The Bermuda Triangle."

The Bermuda Triangle is so far from sailors' minds that it isn't even really on the map. They'd rather not even think about it. Even if a few of them knew, theoretically, that the Bermuda Triangle was out there, they wouldn't be able to find it if they wanted to. They would become lost, possibly forever. For the most part, though, they don't want to try. The Bermuda Triangle is scary and confusing. Sailors hear bad things about it. They'd rather just go around it, staying as far away as humanly possible.

I know that sounds like an exaggeration. And sure, to some extent, it probably is. For instance, there isn't anything about me that is analogous to the Bermuda Triangle's "rogue wave" phenomenon (at least I hope there isn't). I don't capsize sailors, much less entire ships. I keep myself to myself, you know? In fact, I think that's probably what the Bermuda Triangle is up to. It doesn't mean to do any harm, and it's actually pretty nice once you get to know it. It's just that Bermuda doesn't know how to handle itself when somebody sails into its territory, because that hardly ever happens. It hasn't had much chance to practice, and it's used to things going a certain way. So if a sailor DOES come around, it gets a little nervous, freaks the fuck out, and creates hurricane-like devastation in every direction around it. And then it gets embarrassed and sad and calls its friends.

I do not present this theory because I feel sorry for myself. It's just the way things are. Not all of us can be born lighthouses, or nobody would ever get anything done and there would be more sex happening than you could even believe. I just think it's important that I make my Triangular nature clear up front, because later on in the book you might have a hard time believing that a real live person could be capable of such mortifying attempts at romance. You might worry that I don't even realize how terrible I am at basically everything to do with love. So I want you to know that I warned you. I'm aware. I've been collecting evidence for twenty-five years, and now I've gone ahead and documented it here in this book. The conclusions are irrefutable.

My name is Katie Heaney, and I'm a Bermuda Triangle.

As a result, and possibly as a result of other factors like "luck" and "being interested in people who are unavailable and/or terrible for me," I've been single for my entire life. And I don't mean that I haven't had any major long-term relationships, or that I haven't dated anyone in a really long time, or that I've only dated people for a few months at a time. I mean that I have been wholly and totally single for my *entire life*. Not one boyfriend. Not one short-term dating situation. Not one person with whom I regularly hung out and kissed on the face. To be honest I don't even know that I could fairly say that I've been on more than one real date. There were a couple of times when I hung out with a boy I liked and he paid for me and we were both single so I *think* those were dates, but then like a week later he had a girlfriend that wasn't me and I was cursing his very existence, so it's hard to say for sure. But more on that later.

People have interesting reactions when you tell them you've never had a boyfriend and you're over the age of twenty-one. Most girls are pretty good at acting like they aren't shocked, because most of them have at least one friend who doesn't date as much as the others for whom they've learned to be uncondescendingly empathetic. When I'm having one of my "something is seriously wrong with me for being alone" phases (which are, thankfully, relatively infrequent), my friends have learned to conjure up relatives/mythical acquaintances/*Grey's Anatomy* characters who have gone *even longer* than I have without having a boyfriend, so it's totally not weird at all that I haven't had one yet. Practically everybody, except for every last person they can think of at the moment, has been single for as long as I have. My darling, patient friends tell me that I'm still single only because I'm picky, and because I haven't met the right person yet. This would feel truer if I hadn't been shut down by quite so many *wrong* people that I, despite my allegedly high standards, chased after. In any case, it's a nice thought.

Sometimes it feels like this is something I should be worried about. Sometimes, during a couple days every month in particular, I want to spend some time lying on the floor and feeling like there must be something terribly wrong with me. I am at the point in my life where I no longer know another person in my shoes. I could count on my friend Colleen for a long time, but then she had to go and get a pseudo-boyfriend last year. I couldn't believe that. It was almost like she wasn't thinking about how her relationship would affect me.

Most of the time it does not upset me to think about my sad, old, decrepit spinster body. Obviously there are about one trillion things that could be worse about my life. Not having a boyfriend at any given moment bothers me very little. Not having ever had one bothers me only slightly more, only because I want to know that I'll get to fall in love at least once, for real. Not in the way I'm used to, which involves one-sided daydreaming prolonged over embarrassing lengths of time, projected onto boys and men (and Boyz II Men) who either don't know me at all, or who know me but don't exactly *like*-like me. I'm getting too old for that. At least that's what I keep trying to tell myself, right after the latest episode of me acting like some extra-tall preteen with a Justin Bieber problem has passed.

It makes me feel good to know, though, that I am not alone in *every* way. Even if I'm the only permanently single person in my group of friends, or the entire world basically, I'm not the only one to have made a royal mess of my love life. (Can you make a mess out of something that doesn't exist? Yes, actually!) My absolute favorite thing to do is sit around a room with my friends and some wine and remind each other of our worst-ever dating stories. We all screw up. We all keep company with weirdos and assholes. We have all taken too long to realize that something that wasn't even good for us in the first place has ended. That's what I hope this book feels like. You and I are hanging out, and I am drinking too much and talking to you—about my most embarrassing adventures in flirting and kissing and liking boys—for a *really* long time. You are such a good listener. I mean it.

Okay, where do I even begin? Here, let me get you a refill.

Part One

♥   ♥   ♥

THE EARLY YEARS

Heart and Soul

IN 1991 I WAS A KINDERGARTNER at a small Catholic K–12 school in St. Paul, and on the first day, when my mom dropped me off, I cried.

My ability to negotiate successful social relations in those hallways got better, but not by much. For the most part, I kept my head down, my notebooks and my markers arranged in pristine, clinical rows, and my three-inch-long clip-on Polly Pocket earrings on my earlobes. (Only during free time, obviously. Those were the rules.) My report cards all said the same thing: "Smart and shy; a quick learner, but quiet; very, very quiet. A ghost of a student, a whisper on the wind." I'm paraphrasing.

Teachers and parents call any kid that's quiet "shy," but that's not always it. I wasn't shy, I was reserved. I needed time to figure out what the hell was going on with these masses of people running and screaming around me. I wasn't *afraid* of talking to my fellow children. I was simply watching and plotting. I have always chosen my friends from a silent distance, picking them out after a short observation period and only then attempting to get to know them. I couldn't tell you the criteria I use. I just know them when I see them. It's taken years of practice to get it completely right, and it started back in that brightly carpeted kindergarten playroom.

There are really just four things I remember about kindergarten. One, my new best friend was a nice and weird girl named Christy with a big pouf of hair like Hermione Granger's well before any of us knew who Hermione would be. Two, my teacher taught us about segregation by having the brown-eyed kids represent white people and blue- and green-eyed kids represent black people (there were no actual black students in my class), and I and my blue eyes couldn't use the water fountain for like an hour, and everyone cried. Three, I must have looked like a boy, because once I was biking in my neighborhood and an older boy asked me, "Are you a boy or a girl?" and all I could do was say, in an inexplicably apologetic whisper, "Girl."

Four: Cody Williams, heartthrob of the Twin Cities' Catholic elementary school community and probably the surrounding counties as well. My first crush.

There is no love like the love you have for your first crush. There isn't supposed to be, anyway, because your behavior toward your first crush was embarrassing and hopelessly naive. Don't fight me on this. I saw it with my own eyes.

First crushes inspire the sort of shenanigans that would get an older and allegedly wiser person in legal trouble. You can't just go around smacking a person on top of the head just because he has adorable ruddy cheeks, for example. The message that small acts of violence conveyed when you were five will not be conveyed now. You will frighten the person. He will look at you like you're some kind of lunatic, because you are.

First crushes last for years, no matter how they change as you make that all-important transition from age six to age seven, when all of you become harder, somehow. More world-weary. Some kids start out like buttons, or anything else cute that you want to pinch between two fingers, and then they grow up into Mr. Hyde versions of themselves (see: virtually every boy who became a TV or movie star before the age of twelve). These developments cannot touch first crushes. First crushes, in that way, breed resilience.

First crushes, generally speaking, have absurdly American-sounding names, like Mike Smith or Johnny Anderson or Mark Liberty. Sometimes they're so cute and masculine (well, for a child, anyway) that they have two first names. Paul Thomas. Freddy George. Sam Nathan. Look these names up in your elementary yearbook: These are the boys for whom the ink of a million glittery gel pens was spilled.

Thus was Cody Williams.

Everybody—and I mean *everybody*—had a crush on Cody Williams. First crushes and witch hunts are both born this way: out of mass hysteria. Cody, like so many first crushes before and after him, was nonthreateningly cute and *pretty*. He had floppy blond hair, which was ideal, because that way he kind of reminded us of the boys in *Tiger Beat*, who were *all* blond. He was athletic and popular and funny (by six-year-old standards). Again like most other first crushes, we all knew then, on some level, that Cody would never surpass a height of five-foot-six in his adulthood, and that was *okay*. He would always look like Cody Williams, or some slightly off older version of himself. In fact, I just checked on Facebook, and he looks exactly the same. Seriously, it's a little creepy. Like, you could hold his picture from our kindergarten yearbook up to his Facebook picture and you'd promptly forget which picture was which. You'd think they were identical six-year-old twins, one of whom had the genetic-mutant ability to grow facial hair.

So every last one of us loved Cody. We might have had other crushes, too—it was more about quantity than quality in those days, and it's always nice to have a secret—but he was consistently up there on the collective pedestal of my elementary class. My friends and I didn't mind that we all liked the same boy. We bonded over loving him. Cody Williams gave us something to talk about, because six-year-olds don't have real interests aside from double Dutch and Pizza Lunchables. That's a nice thing about little girls, I think—the ability to pin our youthful romantic aspirations on the same little boy, and talk to one another about it, without thinking about it as competition. There was no competition to be had because kids don't have any real end goal to crushes. We called certain people our "boyfriends," but these relationships lasted only days, or sometimes even just a few minutes. Best of all, the same person could be boyfriend or girlfriend to literally dozens of people and nobody cared. It was a simpler life.

Christy and I were both crazy about Cody because we were, after all, alive. We'd sit in the play kitchen under the lofted reading area and watch him across the room, building a fort out of foam bricks with some of the other boys. It was sort of like the 1950s, but with very small people and food that is plastic. Christy and I made ourselves busy pretending that two toy eggs and a piece of rubber lettuce thrown in a bowl result in muffins, imagining ourselves as the joint housewives to our husband, Cody. Sometimes we didn't even pretend like we were cooking, and we'd just sit at the kitchen table and talk about how much we loved him. Across a sea of kids playing with trucks, throwing things at one another, and pretending like they knew how to read (six-year-olds are so *dumb*), we watched him build towers, then kick down towers, and build more towers yet again.

One of the things about Cody that really sealed the deal, heartthrob-wise, was that he was also sensitive. Or, at least, that's what I decided about him based on the revelation that he had musical abilities. Conflating interest/talent in music with emotional maturity and a romantic soul is a mistake that even children make, apparently. Oops!

We had a piano in the kindergarten playroom that went largely untouched, because we weren't supposed to "play" it unless we could *actually* play it, a rule that seemed unjust at the time but that I now understand completely. On a few magical occasions when he needed a break from his normal building-block routine, Cody would sit at the piano and the girls from my class would gather around to listen to him play, because, despite the Catholic school uniforms, we were all shameless hussies. One time Christy and I each draped ourselves over separate ends of the piano, chins resting on our hands and eyes fluttering, like those blond triplets in *Beauty & the Beast* mooning over Gaston. She probably talked me into that one—she was the kind of friend I have always wanted and needed, one who makes me do things I want to do but am too scared to do—but it's also possible that I was involuntarily drawn to the piano's edge by gravitational pull. Cody was playing "Heart and Soul." Both parts at the same time. I mean, come on. I didn't even know that was *possible*.

Cody was also just plain *nice*. He cheered everyone on in gym class, even if they weren't on his team, and even if it was that kid who always ate peanut-butter-and-pickle sandwiches as well as his own snot. When we played T-ball, Cody would yell and clap for every single student who went up to bat, regardless of whether they were able to make contact with the stationary ball (it was harder than you would think). He was just happy for everyone. And because having a cute person say your name aloud is all it takes for most of us to fall in love, having it *yelled enthusiastically* by a cute person pretty much laid waste to our entire grade's female population. It's really no wonder that half the girls in class seemed to want to run to third base after hitting the ball instead of first base. We were all delirious with love *and* youthfully uncoordinated. It was chaos in that gym.

Picture this glorious day with me: Cody standing behind home plate, having just offered to give hands-on batting-stance lessons to anyone who "needed" them, followed by every last girl in kindergarten lining up to his left, suddenly and completely helpless when it came to holding a bat properly. At least half of us were lying. At least half of us played on intramural T-ball leagues and/or had families well versed in teaching us how to play baseball. I stood in line, shaking. Before that day, our main interaction of note went like this:

[Scene: before class has started. Children rowdy. Cody swaggers around classroom, holding imaginary concession case in front of him.]

Cody: "Tootsie Rolls! Whooooo wants a Tootsie Roll? Come and get 'em!"

Me, standing, shrieking accidentally: "I DO!!!!!!!"

Cody, throwing imaginary butts (?) in my direction: "*fart noise*"

Class: "*LAUGHTER*"

I shook off that shameful memory. I mean, how was I

supposed to know that "tootsie roll" was a poop joke? Honestly. I was a *lady*.

I stepped up to the plate, dragging the Wiffle ball bat behind me like, "What's *this* thing, *wink*!" I looked behind me to Cody, who stepped forward on cue. He stood behind me and moved my hands to the "proper" position on the bat—a bit high, to be honest, but I didn't care. This wasn't about baseball anymore. It was about me and Cody, sitting in a tree. K-I-S-S-I-N-G. Hands now in place, Cody pulled a move I like to think was shared with only me and not with the rest of the little girls in my class: He touched my lower back. There is no way for it to not sound inappropriate when I say that he was doing this to "bend me forward into position" but that was the idea. Plus, we were SIX. Don't be so gross.

That experience held me aloft—like an angel, with wings made of heartbeats—for over three years, and I would have kept right on being in love with Cody were we not cruelly separated when my family moved to the suburbs before I started the fifth grade. It was like my parents didn't factor him into their decision to move. I swear to God, we would have dated for at *least* a week within the next couple of years if I had stayed at that school. That back touch really meant something. I'm sure of it, still.

———

As far as I know, there is only one other man ("man," haha) who captivated at least as many girls as Cody Williams did for as many years as Cody Williams did, and that person is Jonathan Taylor Thomas. *Tiger Beat* and *BOP* referred to him as "JTT," and thousands and billions of girls followed suit. "JTT." It still feels good on my tongue.

Ten-year-old JTT starred on *Home Improvement*—a show my parents somewhat reluctantly allowed me to watch with them—in 1991, when I was five. He played the middle son, Randy. Brad, the oldest son, was popular and athletic. Too much of a jock. He also had a mullet, which I found problematic to say the least. Mark, the youngest, was overly sensitive and, later, a goth. Randy was the one for me, a selection that I felt probably set me apart from the undiscerning masses. He was the funny one. His voice was adorable—kind of a drawl without sounding southern, and sort of raspy. He was tan and had sandy brown hair that, no matter how long it got, always looked perfect. I thought he was dreamy, and it turned out that basically every American girl aged five to fourteen agreed with me. I cut out pictures of JTT from *Tiger Beat* and *BOP*, where he was featured on the cover every month, and taped them to my wall. My dad found it hilarious to comment on my JTT collage by asking me, "Who's that kid? Is that that Jonathan Diller-a-Dollar boy?" And I'd be like, "DAD, it's JONATHAN TAYLOR THOMAS! UGH!" And he'd be like, "Oh, Jonathan Bilbo Baggins. Sorry." And I'd be like, "UGHGHGH, DAD!"

My crush on JTT intensified to almost unmanageable heights in 1994, when he voiced the role of young Simba in Disney's *The Lion King*. I was eight at the time, and became convinced that I was able to sing "I Just Can't Wait to Be King" and sound *exactly* like JTT. I am not now nor have I *ever* been able to sing, so my assessment may not have been totally accurate, but it's probably fair enough to say that there wasn't much difference between the pitch of my eight-year-old girl's voice and JTT's then-thirteen-year-old boy's voice. That's just how it works. Anyway, I figured it was a perfect in—if JTT and I were ever to meet, I could sing to him and he'd fall for me. Presumably because he'd be in love with the sound of his own voice, coming out of another person's mouth, I guess.

It's only now, having looked up the YouTube video of this song, that I discovered that JTT did *not* sing young Simba's songs. They were sung by Jason Weaver. At first I was kind of outraged, all, "Who is THAT? Does HE have JTT's wit and sandy-brown hair?" but then I realized Jason Weaver is *also* an actor—he played Marcus on another much-loved sitcom from my childhood, *Smart Guy*. So now it turns out that I have a good in if I ever meet Jonathan Taylor Thomas OR Jason Weaver. Anyway.

Like most good things, my crush on JTT was doomed to end before I could get everything out of it that I hoped for (i.e., a diamond ring). I suppose it was bound to happen eventually, because we grew up to be very different-sized people. Standing as tall as he could, he would likely come up to my nipples, which might *sound* like a good thing but isn't, at least for me. I have a weird need to Google the heights of celebrities I have crushes on to make sure they are at least my height or taller. As if, like, Zac Efron came up to me in real life and asked me out, I'd say, "Ummm sorryyy, no," just because he happens to be five inches shorter than me. (For the record: I would not say no.) It's dumb, but I have to lighten my load somehow. I can't be in love with every hot movie star; it's exhausting. So I sometimes use height to make adjustments to my all-star celebrity crush team where I can, though I've learned that this is a hard game to win at in Hollywood, where the world's most beautiful, tiny little men go to live and work.

A person cannot take the strain of maintaining lifelong

crushes on every last celebrity who has ever graced her adolescent walls. We all have our reasons to let them go: They become sullen drug users, or they come out as gay, or *we* come out as gay, or they go and do something so terrible, so heinous, that we must forget that we were ever attracted to them in the first place. So it was with JTT.

It all fell apart on October 22nd, 1995. Doomsday. The following passage is taken directly from my Mickey Mouse diary from that year. Though it starts off cheerfully enough, do not be fooled. Genuine heartbreak will follow.

Morning Diary! Boy, I slept real good. Listen, have you ever had a crush, and then have it ruined? I have. It was on JTT (short for Jonathan Taylor Thomas). If this stupid "Tom Sawyer" movie would never had [sic] been thought of, this whole thing wouldn't have happened. Anyway, he cut his HAIR! His gorgeos [sic] HAIR! Worse than that, he *likes* it!!!! He said it was better for the heat. (I know that 'cause Christy has a magazine of him.)

Can you believe that? He *cut* his *hair*, without even calling me up to ask what I thought. It was unimaginably cruel, selfish, thoughtless. What was I supposed to imagine running my fingers through now? His stiff little gelled *spikes*? Did he seriously not consider how uncomfortable that would be for me? No, he did not. He didn't think about that because he never thought about me the way I thought about him. That was clear now. I imagine I must have put down my diary and walked around my room, calmly and slowly tearing down the photos of JTT—the old, good JTT, the one who had cared—and throwing them into the trash bin: my first step toward completing the grief cycle that would follow, unabated, for months. Years, even— right up until the appearance on my television of this adorable, bleached-blond-haired boy named Justin, singing to me about how much [He] [Wanted] [Me] Back. That's the other thing about first crushes: There's always someone even cuter coming along, even though you could have sworn it wasn't possible.

I Actually Have More Than One Boyfriend

Two years before I filled my Mickey Mouse diary with angry scribbles about the bad and unforgivable haircut decisions of certain celebrities-who-shall-not-be-named, there was another book I poured my bitter heart into.

Because it was the nineties and I was a girl, my first diary was a Lisa Frank hardcover. The cover depicted two unicorns sort of lovingly poking each other with their rainbow horns, hearts flying everywhere. My entries in it are meticulously dated, so I know that I received it as a gift on my seventh birthday in 1993. The first page provided a "favorites" form to distinguish me from the other carriers of Lisa Frank's lesbian-unicorn model. Most of these "favorites" are no longer accurate, or weren't even accurate at the time: My favorite color, I write, used to be red. My favorite song was "A Whole New World." My alleged favorite sport, soccer (a lie—that was just the one summer I tried to play a team sport), has been crossed out, with the more accurate choice BASEBALL written in a different-colored pen to the side. I would still consider reading among my favorite pastimes, it's true, but I can't say I still hold the same fondness for Joe

Scruggs that my diary states I did back then. He's fine. It's not important.

What matters is that the Lisa Frank diary was the start of a trend.

Ever since then, I have purchased a new diary each time I feel the need to lie profusely to myself for a few weeks or months. Most of these diaries have no more than a third of their pages filled with my writing. I am terrible at keeping them up. I write in them only when I'm obsessing over some guy and want to detail the waning of my optimism. I like to start them right when the fixation has taken hold, when I know enough to be interested and not nearly enough to justify my hopefulness. Then I like to pretend that things are going great for a while. And then I like to track the tragic decline. "Oh well," I write. "Whatever. IT'S NOT A BIG DEAL."

This diary, the Lisa Frank, starts off strong, with bold and declarative statements about Who I Was at age seven, like, "I like school very much. It is fun." and "I sometimes play on the computer." I use innovative and stylistic language devices, pushing the boundaries of the English language with words such as "like'd" and "crazzy." I for some reason keep asking my diary if it also likes all the things I like: "Do you like to swim, Diary? You do? Good!" It's nice to have a friend with common interests.

But what stands out most in my first diary is my repeated and misleading insistence that I had anywhere from one to five boyfriends, at once. (Interestingly, Cody Williams is not among them. His name may not appear in this diary, but I can see him there, in the spaces. The written word was sort of beneath him and me.) What I think I meant by this is that I thought these boys were cute, so I giggled about them, and blushed if they were ever required, for academic reasons, to talk to me. I took mental note of a few small characteristics (like, "brown hair" and "dimples" and "taller than me—for now") and deluded myself into thinking this meant I really knew him. In fact, we were practically dating. Not to alarm anyone, but this pattern of shocking and egregious mischaracterization of the facts started with Lisa Frank and persists in various recycled eco-notebooks *to this very day.*

It all began on November 28th, 1993. After reminding my diary that, seriously, I really like school, I wrote, "I have a boy Friend at school. He is funny. And cute too."

I may have written it in two words with confusing capitalization choices, but I know that I meant boyfriend-boyfriend. And yet: no name. Who was this young man? How did we meet? How was our relationship progressing? Paging through the diary for answers, it takes a while for any clues to come together. The next couple entries are intriguingly dated November 27th, so there's a distinct possibly that at that point in my life I had taken a brief interlude to explore time travel.

My "boyfriend" resurfaces on February 17th, 1994. To mark what appears to have been a nearly three-month-long relationship at that point, I transcribed the following love note: "I have a very cute boyfriend. He is funny. I love Jesus. Oxoxoxoxoxoxoxoxoxoxox." No further remarks as to what Jesus has to do with any of this are included.

The next day, a confession: "I actually have more then one boyfriend and here are there names: Terry, Louie, Will, Jacob. Arn't they nice names? I think they are." If I had any remorse for playing so recklessly with the hearts of four of Minnesota's finest young Catholic school boys, I showed none of it in Lisa Frank's cloudy lavender pages. In fact, over the next several days, I had the nerve to write each of the boys identical love letters in my diary, apparently giving no thought to how the others would feel if they were ever to see them.

On February 19th: "Dear Terry, You mean a lot to me. You are sweet. I love you, Terry."

On February 20th: "Dear Louie, You mean a lot to me. You are sweet. I love you, Louie."

On February 21st: a blank entry, most likely meant to symbolize the inner conflict between my carnal desires and whichever of the Ten Commandments they would violate. Surely I knew I was playing with fire. But could I stop myself?

On February 22nd: "Dear Will, You mean a lot to me. You are sweet. I love you, Will."

On February 23rd: another blank page. Where would I go from here? I had created such a mess in my wake. I knew not where to turn. Could the second grade possibly be any better? It was too far off to tell. For now: only heartbreak. Lust.

On February 24th: "Dear Jacob, You mean a lot to me. You are sweet. I love you, Jacob."

I should note that tucked into the pages of these duplicitous love letters is a valentine. It is, of course, Lisa Frank—a dolphin jumping over the earth (improbable) with the phrase "You Mean the World to Me!" It is from Terry. My preliminary investigation led me to believe that this meant Terry was in the lead in the wholly imaginary race to win my heart, but the next few days reveal shocking news.

February 26th: "Dear Evan, You mean the most to me. You are sweet. I love you the most. Yours truly, Katie....P.S. Sorry about the other boys."

Who was this dashing and debonair outsider? Where had he come from? How had he vanquished the efforts of my four previous suitors? What did he have that the other boys didn't have? Thankfully, I did not need to look much further for the answers to these pressing inquiries.

On February 28th: "Today I'm writing about Evan. Did you know I met Evan at soccer? Well, I did. He is sooooooo cute! He is the cutest boy I've ever seen! There isn't any other boy on earth that is cuter than him! This is my best picture of him." And then there is a drawing of somebody that looks like a cross between Devon Sawa and Gollum, with extraordinarily pointy lips. Would his sharp-looking lips and my lips ever meet? I wanted to know more about this perfect and forgotten boyfriend from my past.

March 1st brought no answers. March 2nd reads "Dear Ghostwriter, please write to me," accompanied by a mysterious drawing of a circle with wavy lines coming off of it. The plot thickens!

March 3rd takes a stab at subtlety, with "EVAN" written across the entire page.

And then, on March 29th, treachery!! A love letter dedicated *not* to Evan, but to Will from before! I insist that *he* is my "best boyfriend," that *he* is the one who is "sooooooo cute," and that it is *him* who I "truly, truly love." If only the priests had known of my scarlet-letter ways, I am sure I would have been banished from elementary school and, quite possibly, the state of Minnesota.

Months passed, as I spent the spring and summer thinking about my life and my mistakes, detailing my sincere love for school, and describing an eye infection. But then, I had a revelation in early August.

August 8th: "Evan is my real Boyfriend! Not Will. Not Louie. Not Jacob. (Ew.) NOT TERRY!!!!!!!!!!!!!!!! Evan is! He is so cute. He Even Like's ME!!! He said I was a great midfield! I met him at soccer. (Ed. Note: There may have been some persistent questioning from the public as to where, in fact, I *really* met Evan. Further research needed.) He is so handsome! I also saw him at swimming lessons! I think He's 6 or 7-year's old. First my boyfriend was Terry. Then Will. NOW EVAN!!!!"

I had had my breakthrough. I was like Diane Lane in *Under the Tuscan Sun*, or Fievel, having successfully Gone West. Evan was the one for me. Not Jacob, not Will, not Louie, and apparently *definitely* not Terry. Soccer brought us together. Soccer would keep us together because I was obviously a stellar midfield. Evan told me so himself. I thought everything was perfect. But soon, the cracks in my rainbow-glass unicorn of dreams started to show.

August 26th: "Evan is just so cute! I'll probably never see him again. Boo-hoo-hoo. Xoxoxoxoxoxoxoxoxoxoxoxoxoxoxoxoxoxoxoxo xoxoxoxoxoxoxoxo. I still love him though."

This ordeal sums up a pattern of behavior I would continue to perfect for about fifteen years. I saw a boy I thought was cute. He took precedence over other male humans with whom I was actually familiar, and to whom I could have actually spoken, if I had wanted. I developed unreasonable assumptions about the direction of our "relationship." I wallowed. I bounced back with impractical enthusiasm. I mistook (or, perhaps, willfully misunderstood) his polite remarks about my athletic "abilities" for a confession of love. He eventually disappeared from my life, and it took me more than a little too long to let it go. (December 1994: "I have a boyfriend too. Like I told you before, his name is Evan.")

I have never played an intramural, unisex team sport since that summer. Sure, this might have something (everything) to do with the fact that I have very little athletic ability and a general unwillingness to risk minor injury—I'd play tennis in high school and college, and I could hit the ball pretty hard and everything, but understand that tennis is an individual sport and I *never* won—but it also has a little something to do with Evan.

I never even knew his last name.

The Bad Girls and Boys

Throughout the latter half of the fourth grade, each day after Catholic school, I changed out of my uniform and into my at-home outfit of choice: a T-shirt with a giant furry spider on it, an unbuttoned red-and-orange flannel shirt over it, and a backward black baseball cap on my head. So it's pretty clear that something troubling and bad was going on inside me. It wasn't puberty, either. I had at least six more years to go before that whole mess.

I think it was rebellion. A small kind, obviously—one that wouldn't challenge my parents or my teachers or any type of authority figure for whom I felt unquestioning respect and unwavering fear, but one that would make me want to look like I was kind of thinking about it. It would have been cooler if my skin-deep transformation had something to do with my transfer from Catholic school to public school, if I had had it up to here with the Man telling me I couldn't wear any colors besides virginal white and...maritime navy, if a nun had rapped my knuckles with a ruler one too many times and I had burst out of my school's doors applying eyeliner with one hand and giving a few whimpering kindergartners the finger with the other, sauntering off into the sunset and, later, into wicked, godless Pine Lake Elementary.

The sad truth is that my Catholic school didn't even HAVE nuns.

All I really had to rebel against, at that point in my life, was myself. I don't think most of us Goody Two-Shoes are as pleased with ourselves as we seem. After all, getting positive feedback from teachers is nice, but having friends who think you're fun is nicer. Good grades were important to me, but the rigidity of my rule-following was a compulsion, not a source of pride. Moving was going to mean starting over, and that was going to have to mean change. After all, I was only just on the very cusp of popularity that previous year, and I had known those girls for over four years. It seemed that liking me took a lot of time. I was worried I wouldn't have enough years to work with when I started my new school, in the last year of elementary. One year was all I'd have before Pine Lake would join up with two other, bigger elementary schools (with even higher proportions of rich and pretty girls, though I did not know this then) in the hellhole that is middle school. I couldn't even get a head start. I didn't even know what public school fifth-graders thought was cool. Drugs, probably. Drugs, fast cars, making out, and other lascivious behavior. I was doomed.

The move to public school was definitely going to mean clothing "freedom," wherein children ruthlessly inflict uniforms upon one another by silently condoning certain clothing brands and styles while prohibiting others. The accessories of popularity (besides the usual glow that comes with being admired by others) at my new, big school in the suburbs could have looked like anything, for all I knew, but I was sure they must be rougher.

It wasn't just going to be Starter jackets anymore. There would be daggers, maybe. Artful facial scars. I didn't know! I couldn't blindly plan for such extremes, obviously, but when the time came, I would be ready to dip a toe into trouble. I wanted to do whatever I had to do to make new friends, just so long as we were only talking about wardrobe adjustments and other social markers that I could ask my mom to buy for me.

The first stage of my transformation came unexpectedly, in the summer between the old school and the new. That's when I fell in love with my first self-evident bad boy. It quickly burned out and was done with in less than a day, but that's just the sort of thing you have to accept when you live life on the edge.

———

I saw him first on the very grand *Titanic*-like staircase inside the foyer of the old, historic-looking St. Paul building where my uncle was holding his wedding reception. The boy was roughly my age, maybe closer to twelve, blond, and adorable. He looked squinty and brooding—like someone who had seen the inside of a principal's office or two. He was wearing a slightly disheveled shirt and tie, and I was wearing a black shirt, a floor-length black silk skirt with white and red flowers on it, and my hair in a half ponytail. It was not my best going-out look. Nevertheless, we made eye contact that smoldered as much as prepubescent eye contact can smolder, which is actually more than you might think. My face was flushed and my pulse quicker. I was dizzy with possibility. We were at a wedding, after all. In fifteen years at our *own* wedding we'd have an amazing story to tell our three hundred guests about how we met.

If I should have been thinking about how we might be

slightly and technically related by that point (he was from my new aunt's side; I hope you give me at least that much credit), I wasn't. I don't think ten- and eleven-year-olds think about that stuff, or at least I hope they don't, because otherwise the fact that my ten-year-old cousin once told six-year-old me that he'd marry me someday when I was "older and prettier" might seem kind of creepy.

The rest of the night was spent like this: I walked around looking for this boy between speeches and meals and bathroom breaks, and when I'd see him I'd look at him, then look away, then look at him again. I never got closer than twenty feet, which is about how far out my anti-flirtation force field has extended since the beginning of my life. When people were dancing, I hovered around the edges of the floor, pretending like I wasn't watching him, but I was. In my mind, he was an impossibly cool dancer. In reality, I think he was just jumping a lot? I don't know. Boys don't have to do anything to be cute on the dance floor if they are cute in the first place. They could just stand there, scowling with their hands in their pockets, and I'd be like, "Aww!"

He looked at me a lot, too, that evening. I am sure of this. Was I the only age-appropriate girl there, and also a person who was intently staring at him every few minutes? Certainly. Was I going to let that diminish my inflating sense of my own appeal? Definitely not. I spent a lot of time doing that thing where you pretend like you're just going about your own business but are actually putting concerted effort into making everything you do a little bit cuter, just in case a certain person happens to be watching. I was all, "Oh I think I'll just bite my lip and twirl my hair a little while I stand here... next to my parents" and "I *always* eat cake this adorably. I am an adorable and dainty eater, just naturally."

After a couple of hours of this exercise in unfulfilled pre-sexual tension, I was forced to leave the wedding reception by my parents. They told my brothers and me that it was time to go, but I asked if we could stay a little bit longer. When they asked why, I think I just told them I was "having fun." They weren't buying it because I was a child at a middle-aged person's wedding reception, so we got our things and headed out. As we walked through the foyer, I saw my true love on the staircase again. He loved that staircase. We locked eyes one last time, but I looked away quickly, because the pain was too much to bear.

This next part is when things got crazy: My family loaded into our car, which was parked across the street. As I buckled my seat belt and looked back longingly toward the house that contained my little blond soul mate, he *ran out onto the porch*. He came to a quick stop, out of breath (I imagine), and looked around wildly. It was like a movie, right when the music would have swelled and everyone in the audience would have started crying because love IS real. He was looking for somebody. Looking for ME.

My parents drove away and I twisted my head around as far as it could go, watching him fade out of sight. "Fate is a cruel mistress," I wish I had whispered aloud to myself.

Some weeks later, at a family gathering, my uncle and new-aunt produced several envelopes of pictures from the wedding and the reception. My heart leaped. I had all but forgotten what the boy looked like, which is what always happens to me when

I think someone is really, really cute. I tore through the photos, probably blatantly uninterested in almost everything: "Yeah, the bridesmaids, cutting the cake, the venue, the cousins, whatever! JUST SHOW ME THAT BOY." Finally, there he was, in profile, at the far edge of a dark photo of the dance floor. I asked my aunt for his name. "Oh that's Tony," she said. "Bit of a trouble-maker." I think that was supposed to dissuade my interest, but I asked for the picture (embarrassing!). "Did you get a chance to meet Jack?" my aunt asked, clearly trying to facilitate a more proper arranged marriage. "He's a very nice boy!" she said, handing me another picture featuring some non-hot ten-year-old. "Um, no, I didn't," I replied, setting the picture aside in the pile with everything else from the wedding I didn't care about.

Tony was pinned to my bulletin board for at least a year after that. His presence carried me through my first year in a new home and a new school, his smoldering gaze the only constant on which I could rely. Under his watchful, semi-glazed eye, I metamorphosed from a quiet, leggings-wearing Catholic school-girl who never broke a single rule into a quiet, oversized-T-shirt-wearing public schoolgirl who also never broke a single rule, but who knew some people that did.

———

What was left of summer after that fateful wedding reception was spent unsuccessfully trying to convert the gazebo behind my family's new home into a neighborhood clubhouse, which I forced on my little brothers and, like, one other younger boy from our block at least five or six times. Weirdly, most little kids do not seem to enjoy having a strict twice-weekly meeting schedule and a mandatory fort-building progress-report policy, no matter *how* many snacks you ply them with. In my alone time, which was plentiful, I sat on my bed in my new room, pretending to smoke cigarettes that I rolled up out of notebook paper (these I would hide, afraid that my parents would learn that I was pretending to smoke pretend cigarettes and would disown me) and envisioning life at Pine Lake Elementary. I was reading Cynthia Voigt's YA novel *Bad Girls*, about two precocious and strong-willed tomboys named Mikey and Margalo. Shortly after I finished the sequel (*Bad, Badder, Baddest*), I started school and met the Mandys.

They were these two kind of punky girls in my class who I noticed—around the edges of our classrooms, the cafeteria, the parking lot where we had recess, always on the edges—and I decided that I, who feared rule-breaking more than death and cried if I ever forgot to bring my homework assignments to class, should befriend them. Mandy #1 was, at age eleven, already five-foot-six and in possession of a decent-sized pair of breasts. She looked sixteen and was hot in a way that made it clear she would be getting into trouble over the next ten to forty years. Mandy #2 was a more normal looking eleven-year-old, save for the blue streaks in her hair, dark lipstick, and very large sweatshirts. Both of them were bratty and sullen, though I always got the feeling that Mandy #2's meanness was more of a display to impress Mandy #1 than something she really meant. Mandy #1 seemed very worth impressing.

I don't remember how the three of us became acquainted because my fifty-five-pound pale little self was not exactly the kind of new kid that makes the other kids whisper in the hallways, "Where is *she* from?" "The wrong side of the tracks, I bet!" At eleven, for me, menstruation was a distant nightmare, and breasts were (to borrow a phrase that should, actually, explain a lot) a Phantom Menace. In any case, we met and hung out at recess, where the Mandys told me about how much they loved Marilyn Manson and The Prodigy. I was like, "Cool, me too, I love those guys."

I didn't have a lot in common with the Mandys, but I so wanted to, because bad girls seemed to me to be the coolest, most unbelievable thing to ever live after my five years in Catholic school. (There are, of course, Catholic bad girls, but it's hard to identify them before the age of thirteen.) I believed, if only briefly, that my daily life could live up to the books I was reading. I wanted things to be different for me in my new school. I wanted to take my own personality and transform it entirely into something that everyone else would not only believe, but would love as well.

It was because of the Mandys that I made my confused and concerned mother buy me boys' Oakley T-shirts, despite never having even seen a snowboard in my life. It was because of the Mandys that I discovered black nail polish and lipstick (and not a moment too soon!). These were little habits and items that were not hard to take on, and for a while it almost seemed like things might really work out for us. Bad, badder, baddest: It didn't matter if I was on the mildest end, as long as I was still a part of the trio.

When I hung out with the Mandys after school, we'd work on designs for our clothing brand, which we called "FROGG." Our "designs" were essentially baggy jeans and T-shirts and sweatshirts, each with a frog logo printed on them. The extra

"G" was just to make it clear that our clothing brand was really cool and unique. We would crowd around my bed with a notepad and colored pencils, and I would insist on drawing the bodies, because I'm bossy. It's not that we had ever grown *closer*, but in the space of these afternoons we would grow apart. Mandy #1 would say something like, "Can't we have a V-neck or something a little lower?" and I'd say, "Umm, haha, I think that would be a liiiiittle inappropriate." We did, however, find common ground in miniature pleather backpacks, which were having what we in fashion liked to call "a moment." Still, we just weren't on the same page, in personality OR in hormonal development. When they left my house, my mom would tell me "those girls need to take a shower." She said, "Their bodies are developing a little quicker than yours, I think. If you know what I mean," and I was like, "MOM!!!!!!!!"

The Mandys went to the local parks after dark to smoke cigarettes with boys three years older than them, which is a thing I had previously believed only happened in YA novels but is actually real. I was never invited to their more dubious extracurriculars, maybe because the Mandys sensed that I was secretly a law-loving nerd who just wanted to make some new friends. It's just as well, because if they had asked me to hang out anywhere where there would be cigarettes—or worse, boys—I would have taken up my standby get-out-of-scary-stuff lie from those days, which was "I have to babysit my brothers." My poor parents. They have no idea how absent I made them sound over the course of my adolescence.

It's hard to explain why I would want to be friends with two people who could have been best described as "kind of asshole-y," but what I think it comes down to is that the Mandys, like bad girls before and after them, just did not give a fuck. This is the opposite of what I do. All I give are fucks. And it seems to me that it might be nice, on occasion, to get rid of some of them. I wanted to shoplift—if only in a theoretical sense, in a world where I knew that I could. I wanted to be able to skip school to hang out with my unbelievably hot boyfriend in a courtyard somewhere. I wanted to inspire fear and fearful admiration.

Bad girls require this intense outward level of confidence, this provoke-me-not attitude that I've never quite been able to muster. At a sleepover once, my friends (later ones, ones I'd made after rehab. Just kidding.) suggested that we watch *Cruel Intentions*. I called my mom to ask her if it was okay if I watched it. She said no. I didn't watch it. I've blocked out what I did instead, or what exactly I told my friends ("Sorry, my mom says that I can't watch rated-R movies until I'm of age"??). The rest of that memory could only be reached through intensive hypnotic regression, I am sure. For another example, in sixth grade, my brief and so-called best friend abandoned me entirely for the new popular girl, and I did nothing. The Mandys would not have let that shit go.

Bad girls don't feel the need to act the way girls are "supposed" to act. They don't wear pretty clothes or subtle pink makeup or waves in their hair. They talk back, often and loudly. They are viciously honest and witty and mean. They are independent and tough. They do things they shouldn't, things that make their parents unhappy and their friends impressed. They don't chase after boys. Boys chase after them. The fictional Mikey and Margalo were like that. The Mandys were like that.

I really ought to make myself a little bracelet that reads "WWTMD?"—What Would the Mandys Do? (Though if

I'm about to do something that one of the Mandys [especially Mandy #1] would do, I should, to be honest, probably not do that thing. I could go to jail.) But maybe that way I'd do something halfway between what the Mandys would do and what I would do. Just a few times, just to know what being bad felt like.

Popular

IN ELEMENTARY SCHOOL, it hadn't really mattered that I wasn't talking to boys and they weren't talking to me. At that age, it's almost like we all know we're pretending when we say we (well, you) are "going out" with someone. We're kidding! We're ELEVEN, for crying out loud.

In middle school, having a boyfriend is not a fucking joke. Nothing is.

Dakota Middle School looked (and looks) like a prison. There is no getting around it. There aren't any windows, the ceilings are low, and the color scheme is this one very specific shade of brown. It should have helped that, in a way, we were all starting there as "new kids"; it was there that kids from Pine Lake joined up with kids from two other local elementary schools, which should have meant there would be more people we didn't know than we did. It's just that some of those suburban kids knew each other already anyway, from their cul-de-sacs and their parents and their sports teams. Some of us were still newer than others.

In the early part of sixth grade I was trying to make my friendship with Kelsey—the first friend I made post-Mandys, who not infrequently tried to convince me that we should "become witches"—work. I also was putting in long hours trying to make friends (defined loosely) with a few kids from the other elementary schools in the district. There was Stacy, who was essentially a human squirrel; Amanda, who was obsessed with jawbreakers and gel pens and, later, would become a cutting, mean-spirited asshole of a child; and Brynn, of whom I remember not one defining characteristic but who had the distinct advantage of being three-dimensional. Look, it's all about opportunity. I was silent, I was small, and I had translucent skin. ("I thought you were allergic to the sun"—a so-called friend.) I had to mine whatever companionship I could from my classmates, my gym partners, and the kids on my bus. I had to find people who would, at the very least, sit with me at lunch, and who were willing to listen to me talk about my newly formed crush on a very popular and adorable boy named Chris who sat near me in Social Studies. I gave up on the idea of friends who would want to hang out with me on the weekends almost instantly. I was too scared to hang out with more than two people at a time, anyway. I figured I would be happy enough spending my free time with books, computer games, and my still somewhat-pliable younger brothers.

I would have been perfectly (mostly) fine just finding people to sit with and talk to. I would have been fine just imagining that the next year would be inexplicably and immeasurably better. (I would, after all, be turning thirteen.) There is no reason for any child to expect to be truly happy in middle school, and although it wasn't as if some of us weren't trying anyway, many of us seemed content to quietly pass the time until things got better. I could keep spending the twenty minutes between arriving at school and the start of my first class sitting in a bathroom stall because I couldn't find anyone in the hallways to talk to. It wasn't ideal, and a lot of people probably thought I had chronic diarrhea, but at least I wouldn't be seen sitting alone in class unfashionably early.

I could have just gotten through my time in that depressing, dimly lit cardboard box of a building, handily avoiding the potential and seemingly life-threatening awkwardness of dances and parties through simple non-invitation. It would have been, if not pleasant, at least easy. But then they—the adults, who meant well but knew nothing—went and forced a social life upon us. They made us put on roller skates.

———

First we had to do it in gym class. We watched a safety video and got a quick lesson before tying up disgusting old roller skates (the four-wheel kind) and heading out across the wooden gym floor, in lap after lap, for forty minutes. Never mind that it was no longer 1960 and all of us had Rollerblades at home—this was physical education. It was about suffering, and confusion, and lowering our already dying self-esteem.

We only skated in circles. Sometimes when the gym teachers felt that we were getting a little too good a hang of it, they'd blow a whistle and turn off the music, and everyone would have to turn around and skate in the other direction. This was allegedly done so that we worked the muscles on the other side of our bodies, but I think it was really so that the teachers could watch us try to scramble to a stop and turn around quickly enough before they restarted the music. There were always casualties. Naturally, they were *never* the popular kids who, in addition to having nice hair and clothes, were apparently gifted by God or physics with the natural ability to glide.

Everyone tried to skate with their friends, which created traffic issues as well as a growing and panicky sense of isolation and hopelessness. It was hard enough to find friends in that hellscape when we were standing stationary at our lockers or sitting in the cafeteria, let alone when we were all flying around the gym on wheels. It was hard to keep up because I was scrawny and had very little athletic finesse, and it was also hard to keep up because none of the people I was pretending to be friends with were actually interested in having me skate by them. So I mostly skated by myself. It was the most tragic thing ever, except for the time when a boy skate-pushed me into the wall for no apparent reason. ("He probably likes you"—an idiot.) That was even sadder.

As if this were not enough, the overlords at Dakota Middle School decided that we should put our practice to good use with enforced socializing in the form of semi-annual trips to Saints North roller rink. Everyone understood that these trips were a very big deal. Field trips are widely considered to be a marked improvement over normal school life, but, being absent of any semblance of educational purpose, trips to Saints North were, in theory, the absolute best. If you had solid friends and especially if you had a boyfriend or girlfriend, they probably *were* the best. For everyone else, it was jittery stress and excitement—dread and nachos and the rush of hopeful adrenaline combined.

On the trips we were granted a few hours to skate—or, mercifully, Rollerblade—under disco balls and strobe lighting, accompanied by the most important music of our time: Savage Garden, Backstreet Boys, and Brandy. We brought cash from our parents and spent it mostly on candy and on this really great, sticky-sweet rollerball lip gloss they had. Most importantly, we tried to skate with cute boys.

There were chaperones, presumably, but I do not remember ever seeing one. Perhaps they felt, mistakenly, that nothing all that bad could happen in a roller rink. For future reference: Roller-skating field trips are the middle school equivalent of a booze cruise, except that instead of alcohol we were drunk on dozens—*dozens*—of Pixy Stix. Everyone fought with each other and girls cried in the bathroom. Boys broke things (How do you break things on a vast expanse of empty floor? Ask a twelve-year-old boy) and leered at the popular girls. Everyone yelled the entire time. We grew accustomed to the darkness and the enclosed space and accepted it as our new home. We lived there now. Would we ever get out? We doubted it. We went into the laser-tag room, paranoid and delirious, and shot at one another. It was a little like *The Lord of the Flies*, but with more 98 Degrees.

At the very first sixth-grade trip to Saints North, I decided that if I was going to be forced to be social in the dark with my classmates, I might as well be on a suicide mission. I wanted to skate with Chris from Social Studies and, in doing so, cement our future together. A future in which I would be popular—not because I necessarily liked (or knew) any of the popular kids themselves, but because having such a large, built-in group came with so many obvious perks. For one, I wouldn't have had to worry about goddamn Saints North.

In my mind, my chances with Chris that day were fair to middling. True, I was not friends with any of the popular girls, much less the boys. True, my hair was stupid. But on the other hand, we had at least spoken to each other before, in class. I had even made him laugh once or twice. I was wearing my favorite T-shirt. He didn't have a girlfriend that week. What could go wrong? (Everything.)

Mixed in with the other hot late-nineties jams, Saints North always played two couples' songs, before the first of which they'd make an announcement that the boys should ask a special girl to skate. The second couples' song was called the "Snowball," in which the girl asked the boy, but we all knew that the Snowball was a bunch of bullshit. If you wanted it to mean anything, the asking had to be done by the boy. Snowball was only for girlfriends to ask their boyfriends to skate after they'd already skated together for the *real* couples' song. Frankly, it was a little unseemly in any other scenario. I don't know where we learned all these regulations or why we were all so sexist, but that is just how middle school works, and it's terrible. Everybody should sit at home from ages eleven to fourteen. People at that age are too mean and weird and dumb to be let out in public.

Because nobody talks to each other directly about anything in middle school, I planned to have Kelsey ask Chris if he'd ask me to skate during the *real* couples' song. *He* needed to ask *me*. (I realize now that I should have asked her to magic this event into existence using her witchcraft expertise. It could not have hurt.) This, sadly, is among the bravest things I've ever done. I don't really know what I was thinking. I must have talked myself into a now-or-never-type ultimatum, wherein I knew my chances in the confines of our actual school were slim to none, but my chances in a disco-lit roller rink were marginally better only because nobody knew what was going on out there on the floor. It was all hormones and chaos! I could practically just skate up alongside him and grab his hand and he'd just be thankful for the extra support, maybe. But I wasn't about to go crazy—this was a process.

I gathered my team into a huddle by the lockers. "Okay, tell me exactly what you're going to say," I told Kelsey. Stacy and I leaned closer to her, waiting for the plan. "Ummm, I'll just be like, 'Do you want to skate with Katie?'" said Kelsey. I rolled my eyes. "Oh my gosh, Kelsey, you can't be so obvious about it. You have to like, be casual." She looked confused, probably because I was making no sense. I was already starting to sweat and shake a little bit. But it was too late to turn back. "Ask him if he is asking anyone to skate for the couples' song. And *then* if he says no, *then* you can ask him if he'd ask me. Then come find me and tell me what he said," I said. I felt like I was going to throw up. I put on thirty coats of apple-flavored rollerball lip gloss really quickly to try to calm down. "Fine. That's what I'll say. Okay I'm going over there!" said Kelsey. "Wait, noooooooooooooo!" I screamed. "Too late. I'm going," she said, because middle school kids are the worst.

I ran to the bathroom and went about pretending to fix my hair, even though that damn ear-length bob was really beyond repair. I paced. When the door opened, I'd wash my hands. I had washed my hands about five times for about a billion hours total before, finally, the door opened to reveal Kelsey and Stacy and my future and my fate.

"WHAT DID HE SAY?" I stage-whispered, but I already knew. They hadn't come in the door squealing and giggling, so the news couldn't be good.

"He said he'd skate with you if you asked him for Snowball," said Kelsey, her head drooped to the side in mock empathy (middle school kids aren't capable of real empathy). "I'm sorryyyyy," she said, frowning. Then she turned around and left, presumably to get out before I could kill her.

Stacy stayed on because she was a little bit nicer than Kelsey. She sat with me on the floor while I tried not to cry. I hid in the bathroom for the rest of the field trip. I didn't want to risk the chance of going out there and seeing him skating with another girl, or seeing him laughing with his friends, or seeing him in really any situation that wasn't him confessing his love for me. Nor did I want him to see me, ever again, because then he'd have to look at me, and looking at me would almost definitely mean that he'd remember what I'd done and feel either amused or, worse, pitying. As if I weren't taking the news hard enough, I had to go and hear *NSYNC's "(God Must Have Spent) A Little More Time On You" playing through the wall. It basically felt like Justin Timberlake himself was standing over me, pointing and laughing and wearing a wallet chain.

I can clearly see now that Chris's answer wasn't as bad as it seemed that day. After all, he had expressed a willingness to skate next to me, to be linked with me *publicly*, if only I would ask him. Sure, he was probably just being a polite kid. But to risk upsetting the totem pole of popularity just for the sake of being friendly? That was practically unheard of. Social groups meant something. They determined who you could eat with, who you would huddle around lockers with before school, whose birthday parties you could expect to be invited to without transgressing social norms. They determined who you could go out with, and who you could reasonably ask to the school dances. They were everything.

I was groupless. I could see that even more clearly now.

I should have known better than to "go after" Chris, who,

because he was popular, had his pick from dozens of girls whose temporal distance from breast development was nearly a decade shorter than mine. And it didn't matter if he thought I was nice or funny or even pretty: It was just not going to happen. I had two choices. I could move forward with my life, unconcerned by the social standing of myself and others, moving freely and pro-actively among cliques to form my own group of friends unin-terested in emulating the cool girls or dating the cool boys. Or I could still quietly care, for a few more years, even though I'd pretend I totally didn't.

———————

On my first day of seventh grade, in Earth Science, I was assigned to sit in a chair next to Nicole Barrett, who was blond, pretty, athletic, and tomboyish, as well as unusually popular in her own right. Nicole Barrett didn't even seem to hang out with most of the popular girls most of the time, though she certainly could whenever she wanted to. Her popularity seemed indepen-dent from that of the popular girls—she somehow made her sitting at their lunch table (her lunch table, really) seem like a favor. I don't know how to explain it. She could do whatever she wanted, and one of those things was—at times, during in-class lab work for the most part, and in a way that made me feel like I was really *helping*—copying my worksheets, which I let her do because I wanted to be her friend as soon as I met her.

It isn't true that letting people copy your homework makes you popular, but it definitely doesn't hurt. This, among hand-fuls of invaluable, now forgotten information about rocks, is what I went on to learn in Earth Science.

For group rock-related work our little seating pod would join with the desk in front of ours, where two popular boys—Mike and TJ—sat. Mike and TJ copied work off of Nicole's copy of my work. This is the circle of life. Sometimes Nicole's friend Erin (who sat at a table to our right) would join our group, when her table mate was absent or when our teacher was feeling particularly amenable to the charms of pretty thirteen-year-old girls. Then the four of them would talk about the things that popular kids talked about (nothing), and I would listen and feel at once extremely included (physical proximity–wise) and very much alone (everything else–wise). Yes, I was sitting RIGHT there, but that didn't mean anyone had to say anything to me, or that I had the right to say anything to them.

On one such occasion TJ turned around in his chair and said to Nicole, "You have Grand Tetons." Then he and Mike snickered. We had, I suppose, been learning about mountain ranges recently, so the comment was not entirely without scholastic merit. He looked over at Erin and noted, "And you have Regular Tetons." They all giggled some more, and I made myself very busy filling in that day's worksheet, shifting my upper arms to cover as much of my torso as possible, writing with spindly, contracted arms the same way a *Tyrannosaurus rex* might. Ignoring me, in that scenario, was really more of a favor than it was anything malicious. (Obviously, to have none of it said at all would have been the ideal, but this *was* middle school.) We all knew that there were only a handful of terrains and global regions with which one's chest area could be semi-accurately described, and that neither "Great Plains" nor "Arctic Tundra" were particularly flattering.

So I wasn't exactly making great inroads with TJ or Mike or Erin, but that was fine. Nicole was the one who mattered.

At first my wanting to be her friend must have had something to do with popularity, and a little of *that* must have had something to do, still, with Chris. It's not that anyone outside the group ever knows much about the popular kids themselves, or what they do when they hang out on the weekends (though we hear it's trouble), or even what they talk about at lunch. It's that we see a large and unshakeable network—with stars like Nicole, yes, but still a unified front—a practically infinite number of people to potentially have over after school, limitless in-crowd dating possibilities (it always seemed like a game of Go Fish, but with people), and people to sit and stand with. That last one, actually, is really the most important. Middle school is three years spent worrying whom to sit and stand with.

If I could have had a group as big as theirs—and theirs was huge: twenty, thirty blessed children—statistics would have been in my favor, and at least a few of them would have landed in my lunch period. At least a few of them would have gotten to school when I did, and I wouldn't have had to dart to and from the bathroom in the morning. It wasn't about wanting mass approval as much as it was wishing to no longer be exhausted.

For me, and for a lot of kids, I think, the popularity myth—the idea that there's something inherently and unbreakably superior about these people—ended as soon as I realized I didn't hate them. In seventh grade, I found out they were nice and normal. Well, *some* of them were nice and normal. Let's not get carried away.

What happened is that I made friends with some popular girls, and absolutely nothing changed.

With Nicole it started through little notes we exchanged during class, me holding my notebook on my knee and writing something to her—about how weird our teacher was, or how boring the rocks were that day—and her carefully taking the notebook from me and writing something back. Then our friendship began to seep out of the Earth Science room and into the hallways, where we started stopping briefly to say hi when we saw each other between other classes, and even sometimes in the cafeteria. When she broke her leg playing soccer, she chose me (at least some of the time) to be the one to fulfill this weird, unwritten policy our school had in which an injured party got to leave class five minutes early, accompanied by a friend who would carry her backpack and drop her off at her next class before normal passing time made hallway traffic unmanageable. I became, for the first time of many, the skinny sidekick to a cool and collected blond bombshell—girls I'm drawn to because they're different, because they know things I don't, and because their first impulse is to create fun. Girls like Nicole essentially made me have a social life. Girls like Nicole made me less afraid of everything.

It was through our notes and our hallway walks that I learned the details about Nicole's older, eighth-grader boyfriend (something the standard popular girls only dreamed of), who was cute, wealthy, and popular, and who was on track to play varsity basketball in high school. They only kissed, she assured me, but she *had* sat on his lap a few times when they were hanging out after school. (This scandalized me for several days, but this is the kind of thing these girls help me with: adjusting my societal normalcy scale.) His name was Billy. Billy, as it happened, rode the same bus I did, and once it became known that I was kind of friends with his girlfriend, he started giving me obligatory little waves or half-smiles when he got on in the mornings.

Then, cruelly and out of nowhere, Billy dumped Nicole for a girl in his own grade. It doesn't matter who it was, because she was so obviously inferior to Nicole Barrett that to describe her in any way would be to give her more humanity than she deserves. Everyone could see that, except for Billy, because he was a brainless, spineless, dopey-faced idiot with poor vision and no soul. These are the things I wrote to her in class to try to make her feel better, and on some days, it worked. But Nicole stayed depressed for a while, until she became livid instead. She had been dumped while she was on crutches, which we agreed seemed pretty unfair. We went over to her house after school and ate cookie dough and talked about how stupid Billy was, how she could do so much better, and how neither of us necessarily wished that he would die, but that neither of us would be all that upset about it if it happened naturally, like in gym or something.

At some point during this early stage of recovery, Nicole started referring to Billy by the pseudonym "Nutsak," which I believe is something she learned from her older brother, and I started drawing her little stick-figure comic strips about his demise. I called them "Adventures of SuperKatie" and their plots were slight variations on this theme: My winged heroine character (SuperKatie) would witness Nutsak/Billy saying something terrible to Nicole, or being generally moronic in her presence, and I would fly in to save her, subsequently beating the shit out of him in any number of comically exaggerated ways. Nicole often helped, but it was usually me who did the heavy lifting, destruction-wise. Victory and vengeance were inevitable in six panels or less. It's not the most subtle way I've ever attempted to demonstrate my indispensability as a best friend, but anyway it made her laugh.

Nicole even showed the comics to another friend of hers, Christine (another singularly popular girl, with naturally white-blond hair and adorable button features), and that's how the two of them decided that if they were ever, in a doomsday fantasy world, to take drastic action against the bus that harbored both "Nutsak" and myself, they would make sure to get me off safely first. When they told me this in the hall one day, I felt that belonging I'd been missing since my family moved to the suburbs. Nicole and Christine and I started talking about organizing a "Crew," which was this sort of *West Side Story* scenario we envisioned in which she and a large group of her friends confronted Billy in the hall and threatened him into shameful retreat. That was about as fleshed out as this idea ever got, so I should have known better than to hope that Nicole meant it when she said we should all make shirts that said THE CREW on them. I also should have known better than to become so committed that I drew designs for them in my notebook.

(It has often been hard for me to know if people are serious when they talk about making T-shirts. Just to be clear: Nobody ever means it, ever. Making and wearing matching, themed T-shirts is embarrassing. Unless you want to make some with me right now, or something.)

It would have been nice to have that visual cue of togetherness. I imagine it would have felt like being part of one of those annoying families that wear matching family shirts when they travel to amusement parks together so they don't "get lost," but obviously inestimably cooler.

We did it without matching clothes of any kind, but Nicole and I stayed good friends through middle school, and even a little into high school. Christine and I, too. She slept over at my house and we were partners in class projects whenever we could be. She once told me her brother was possessed by a demon, and that was the second time I realized these people were not only normal (in the sense that they were abnormal, like the rest of us), but that some of them might even be seriously strange. Beautiful, but strange. Some of the others were exactly as boring as everyone else, in a way that was both a huge relief and a little depressing. A few were not very smart. Most were. A few were not very nice. Most were. All of them had great hair. (Most girls do, though, right? Girls: We're nailing it, hair-wise.) Anyway, it felt like something I should have known forever but still took thirteen (or fourteen) years to figure out: Girls are nothing to be afraid of, no matter the kind.

Boys, on the other hand.

Part Two

♥   ♥   ♥

HIGH SCHOOL

The Beginning and the End

IN MIDDLE SCHOOL, braces had seemed like the great equalizer. It's not that certain people didn't look better in them than others—certain kids, i.e., the popular ones, always seemed to look somehow *more* attractive when they first got braces, possibly because it made them even shinier. That part wasn't fair. But at least we all had them, and in that way, the misery was shared.

By my freshman year of high school, things didn't seem so equal anymore.

Suspiciously, all the popular kids—who would retain that label, "popular," well beyond the point at which anyone lent it any credibility, and who will probably be referred to as such at our fifty-year class reunion—got their braces off first, sometime over that transitional summer. (Was our orthodontist... *in* on this?) It's already ridiculous how good popular kids look on the first day of school. They are tan, they are older-looking, they have an effortlessly casual and stylish first-day outfit. Now, too, they had white, straight, naked teeth. They were laughing and smiling more than they really needed to, in my opinion. I, meanwhile, had six months left to go. I still had binders, those extra bands that bound my top teeth and bottom teeth closer together and punished me for talking. *I* still had headgear. I didn't have to wear it to school, but I might as well have.

Here's the way I looked at fourteen: exactly the same as I did at thirteen, and twelve, and eleven.

My hair was still parted down the middle, and still ear-length, and I was still very skinny. Skinnier, even. I weighed ninety pounds and was about five-five—the same body I'd had throughout middle school, but stretched, like someone had grasped my head and my feet and pulled me, like one of those rubbery dolls filled with sand. I was still so perfectly flat on both sides of my body that if I turned sideways, and if the lighting was just right, I would disappear. I could have used that power for great evil, had I not still, also, been insufferably well behaved, rigid, and frightened.

All of this sort of made it hard to see high school as the start of something grand and new, even though the hope that it would be is what had gotten me through middle school. My first day, delayed two weeks by construction on our high school, was anticlimactic. (My locker was not next to the locker of the hottest boy in school; nobody put a solitary red rose on my homeroom desk; I was not invited to sit with seniors at lunch. It was all a bunch of bullshit.) First days of school always are, really. They are like New Year's Eve and Valentine's Day: You can't help but hope they will be a little more charmed, like a movie, or like a story you once heard about someone else. They never are. They are just days.

Second days, though. Second days can be surprising.

———

I hovered outside math class, waiting to go in until I really, really had to. I knew from day one—yesterday—that my decision to take "Squeeze" Math (a class on the intensive track that combined Algebra II and Advanced Geometry into one hellish hour a day) was a poor one, and not just because I hated math more than anything in life. I also hated my teacher with an instant and intensive spirit. You know those high school teachers who so quintessentially and stereotypically embody their subject matter that it is as if they were cast by a director? Mr. Carter was like that. I did not know they still made glasses like his glasses. He told us his dog was named "Dooty," short for Dooty Dexy, which is a phoneticized version of the calculus formula for second derivatives. Also, he was terrifying. He called on people whom he suspected of not knowing the answers, humiliated tardy students, and had a penchant for tickling that I would call borderline inappropriate, at best. Math nerds *loved* him.

My seat assignment put me across the table from this other freshman girl, Leigh, who seemed smart and funny, who wore her blond hair twisted into little Gwen Stefani–esque faux dreadlocks, and who I had decided I'd try to befriend. So that second day, I was trying very hard (too hard) to be relaxed and calm and carefree. I was trying to seem like someone a cool girl would want to be friends with.

Mr. Carter was going over our homework (because one does not go without homework on a first day from a teacher like that), and the rest of the class was quiet and attentive. I leaned back in my navy, plastic, piece-of-shit chair, reclining against the windowed wall next to my group's table. Plastic met worn plaster and, for a second, everything was totally fine—I was very relaxed and casual. Then the hold vanished, and my chair slid and scraped all the way to the ground, and I went right along with it. The legs were metal and the floor was, seemingly, noise-enhancing tile. It was the one moment in my life thus far that truly deserved the label "cacophonous." This was the stupidest, loudest, dumbest chair. I can't emphasize that enough.

When I got up off the floor, picked up my awful chair, and quickly sat down again, while the entire class (which, by the way, contained a fair number of sophomores and even a few juniors) watched me in disappointed, disgusted silence, this is the look I tried to convey with my face: "Can you believe this CHAIR?" I looked over at Leigh, hoping for something like sympathy or reassurance or, maybe, a standing proclamation about the notorious unreliability of our school system's cheap furniture, but instead she looked away.

I probably would have done the same thing. (When you are an early teenager, there is nothing more embarrassing than being kind to someone who is embarrassed.) That didn't mean it didn't hurt, in every sense. Worst of all, this was back when I still had the fear of a Catholic God in me, and, worse still, the fear of my probably equally omniscient parents. This was before I'd given myself permission to swear. The only comfort I could give myself was in the form of a small, whispered, "*Shoot.*"

My high school had a rotating seven-class, six-period schedule, in which one class was shifted throughout the day and then skipped once a week. It was very confusing, and an unnecessary added stress for someone who was already relying on a map (a printed-out, highlighted MAP) to find her way to class. (Sure, a few other kids used one on the first day, but did I really *have* to use it the whole week? Was not being lost *worth* it?) So I hadn't had U.S. History that first day. I didn't have any reason to believe I should look forward to it when I speed-walked there after Math that fateful second day, either. I just wanted to go home. History would be my last class of the day, at least, and though I wanted to believe things couldn't get worse, my personal experience suggested that there would always be room for new and interesting forms of humiliation.

There are so few people who can make your cheeks hot without looking at you or talking to you or even knowing you are there. Normally, I think, infatuated cheek heat is a response to personal attention. I've been head over heels without information or cause many times since, but I don't think anybody has made me swoon so cartoonishly as Jake Myers did when he walked into history class ten minutes later.

It was always easiest to fall in love with boys in those first few days of school. Scientifically speaking, this can most likely be attributed to the fact that, at that point, they are still working through the new school outfits their moms and/or older sisters picked out for them, and have yet to regress to their sweatpants and sports-team T-shirts. It's not that loving a boy who wears holey sweatpants and a dirty T-shirt in public is impossible; it's just that it makes it harder to muster *quite* as much enthusiasm. But Jake, on that day so early on in the year, was wearing jeans and a plaid, button-down shirt. This, by the way, is all it has ever taken for a boy to look great. Two pieces of clothing. They could look like almost anything. (It is so simple. And yet!) I didn't notice his shoes, because generally I find that that area is best overlooked and excused.

I didn't know it yet, but he would become one of our high school's super-athletes. There were hints of athletic (and, presumably, sexual) prowess there. For one, boys as ridiculously

Abercrombie-esque good-looking as he was are always sports stars throughout high school. It is a rule, a self-fulfilling prophecy. It seems as if, sometime during elementary school, coaches make note of the little boys with the most classic bone structure and the best height projections and kidnap them, training them under cover of night. Not all of them will make it in college ball (that's what people call it, right?) because by the time they're all seniors, many of them will have been riding more on the sportsman-like nature of their faces than their actual abilities. But until that day, coaches will keep putting them on the field in the most prominent and visually appealing positions because they just kind of *look* like that's where they should be.

At least I'm pretty sure that is what's going on.

Every year before that one (and for a number of years after, too) I told myself that the next year would be different, boy-wise. When I was twelve I thought that turning thirteen would mean I would just naturally get a boyfriend, because I'd be thirteen. When that didn't happen, I told myself that when I was fourteen and a freshman in high school, *then* I would get a boyfriend. I don't know how to explain this logic, except for that when you toss a coin in the air nine times in a row, and they all land on the ground as tails, you just sort of figure that the tenth one has to be a head. (Even though this is not technically true in *actual* probability! Because no one toss depends on the previous tosses' outcomes! Statistics is my one really good area of math. I just abuse it sometimes.) On some level I knew that the laws of probability did not apply to real life in almost any way, and especially not in high school. But I also kind of thought they might.

So when Jake walked into my history class that day, and my

face went hot (in almost exactly the way it does when you're embarrassed, but with noticeably more hope), and I developed a sudden and irreversible obsession based not only on how he looked, but on an entire personality that my mind both created and believed to be true, I have to believe it had at least something to do with my (mistaken, unrealistic) coin-toss theory.

Due to the miracle of assigned group work, I was paired up with Jake in history class for a few projects. Over the course of that first semester, I learned that my capacity to project desired qualities onto an attractive person was even more advanced than I had previously thought. For instance: I decided, after approximately ten minutes of interaction and witnessing Jake correctly answer a question ONCE in class, that he was a genius. "Seriously, he seems really smart," I whispered to any of the girls sitting near me in any of my other classes. "It's not JUST that he's incredibly hot and athletically gifted. He is also extremely intelligent, and probably also funny. He looks like he'd have a really good sense of humor." They nodded. They had no idea what I was talking about, but they nodded.

Aside from our (mandatory) classroom interaction, the only other exchange I had with Jake took place a few weeks into the semester, in the lunch line in the cafeteria. I was waiting alone when I felt someone poke my shoulder. I turned around and was stunned—STUNNED—to see that, barring any kind of ceiling robotic-arm trickery, it appeared that it was Jake who had touched me. On my shoulder. With the fingers. On his hand.

I don't remember it exactly, but this is roughly how the conversation went:

"Hey," he said, smiling giant and amazing.

"Hi!" I said. "How are you?"

"Pretty good. What about you?"

"Pretty good."

Then I turned around without saying another word. I don't know why. It didn't occur to me to do or say anything else. We were in line, I suppose, and it felt like it would be weird to just keep facing backward like that, and also what else did we have to talk about? Nothing. I knew it to be true, but I also didn't care or necessarily realize it on a practical level. An inability (and an unwillingness) to talk to the subject in question just isn't the sort of thing I was going to let dissuade me from obsessive infatuation.

After that first semester, when U.S. History ended and no other force of good stepped forward to put Jake and me in a shared classroom once more, there stopped being a real reason for us to say hi to each other in the hallways. This is how high school operates: You don't say hi, even to people you know, unless you have a good goddamn reason. I kept hoping for a new excuse to show up—maybe I'd find his misplaced biology folder, or the thirty-odd people with last names that separated Jake's locker and my locker would be suddenly expelled.

In the meantime, I spent my weekdays telling my friends (or really anyone who sat near enough to me in any of my classes) that I had a crush on Jake Myers, and I spent my evenings imagining him a personality befitting of such embarrassing, frequent praise. The thing is, when I talked to girls about Jake, I sometimes told them I had a crush on someone I nicknamed "Alpha Omega," as in the beginning and the end, as in God. (It was my last year of weeknight religious education classes, and I was applying my course material inappropriately.) I successfully forgot about that part of the story for a number of years, but the last time I looked at my freshman yearbook, I saw a message from a girl in my math class that reads, "Having math class with you was so fun! Alpha Omega, haha wow, good times." Haha, wow. Good times.

They all knew who "Alpha Omega" stood for, too. I'd ask every girl who she had a crush on, and she wouldn't tell me, and she'd ask me who I had a crush on, and I'd say, "Ohhh, haha, well, I call him Alpha Omega." Then she'd say, "Who is that," and I'd tell her right away, because I can't keep my own secrets secret. (Obviously.) It sort of undid the whole point of having a code name in the first place. But your first mistake was thinking that anything I did in high school would ever make sense.

It went on like this for a year and a half.

———

Now that I am older, and it is over ten years since I last felt in love with a boy I called Jesus Christ, I feel like I need to apologize and explain myself. I'm sorry, I was being ridiculous. Pretend I never even said anything. Pretend I was never here.

If I were on the stand in a courtroom, testifying in my own defense, now would be the part where I'd lean over the bench to pull the fabric off the easel I set up before court. I'd say, "Ladies and gentlemen of the jury: Exhibit A." Under the sheet would be a poster displaying a screenshot of The Sims. I was playing The Sims a lot back then. I mean it: a lot. When I was hanging out with my friends (almost always one-on-one, with girls I culled from math class), I was usually either a) talking to them about Jake, b) playing The Sims with them, or c) grotesque combinations of all the above. This means that I was making them watch me play The Sims *and* talking to them about a boy I didn't know. I'm sorry about that, too.

In The Sims it takes ten minutes to make someone your boyfriend. Here's what you click on, with slight variations depending on shared Sim interests: Talk, Talk, Talk, Joke, Talk, Hug, Talk, Talk, Flirt. Joke, Talk, Flirt, Hug, Flirt, Talk. Flirt, Kiss. Kiss, Kiss, Kiss, Make out. You just keep clicking, and the other Sim basically can't leave unless you do something extremely weird, but it's hard to do something extremely weird because certain dialogue options only become available to you as the other Sim grows more receptive to them. Unless you really do not understand basic models of human conversation, your Sim can date whomever she wants. It's so easy that it's boring, but in a nice way. So you might invite a third Sim over and flirt with him in front of your boyfriend, and then make out with him in front of your boyfriend, and watch him stomp his feet and gesture at you as if to say, "I am literally right here in your kitchen. I just picked up your dirty plates off the floor and put them in the sink, and I turn around to see you and George Sim cheating on me in front of my face?" And you are like, "Yeah," and you marry George in front of him, too, and it's so easy, so you start wooing girls and the elderly and your married neighbors, and the weirdest part is that when you marry each of them in the backyard, all your exes just show up. They seem happy for you, too, because they're clapping.

But then it gets out of hand, and you start over, and this time you swear you'll be nice. You make and marry your crush all over again, and you have kids together. But then you quit your job, and while your husband is at work robbing banks, you wander the neighborhood seducing everything. Still, that first part is always so nice.

All of my Sims eventually became callous, adulterous, pan-sexual nymphomaniacs because it was easy and because, even on the computer, my dream Sim life with my dream Sim boyfriend seemed a bit too shallow to be true. (It's also the way the game sets you up to be, because you need so many friends to succeed in your job, and people like you much longer, with much less effort, if they're in love with you. Which . . . is exactly like real life, maybe. Whoa. Is it? I actually don't know, but it sounds familiar.) It was around that age, too, that my imagination was starting to go. I kept trying anyway.

If you're looking at me sarcastically, like, "Wow, are you try-ing to tell me you developed a virtual life wildly different from your own, and in that virtual life you often carried out your inner fantasies as well as your fears, Catholicism-based guilts, and behaviors otherwise unacceptable in everyday society? No. Way," then, yeah, I know. Most of what I did in the early part of high school is most of what most people do in (at the very least) the early part of high school: imagine that it could have gone differently. It could have landed somewhere between what I really did and what my computer use indicated I wanted. That would have been fine. I was willing to compromise.

I don't know when I stopped loving my ideas about Jake, but crushes like that always start and end so definitively. One day I'm in love and, bam, just six or seven hundred days later, I'm not. Who knows why, exactly: It can't have had anything to do with him, because I didn't know anything about him. I still don't. I guess that must mean it had something to do with me, and though I'd like to say it was because I grew up between the ages of fourteen and sixteen, that doesn't sound quite right either.

Still, Jake Myers, my Alpha and Omega, would be the last crush I'd ever have that I did literally nothing about. Yes, there would be a range of near-nothingness, effort-wise, for a while. Almost nothing, kind of nothing, basically nothing. But never again just nothing nothing. So that was something.

Will There Be Drinking?

AFTER SPENDING THE FIRST TWO YEARS of high school like I spent the eight years before—hanging out with a random assortment of girls, never more than one at a time, usually holed away in her basement or mine, like mole people with braces watching *Clueless*—I started junior year with a group. Leigh and I had, despite first impressions, gotten close during the previous year. She was too funny to write off—such a skilled gossiper and storyteller, the kind of girl I always want to impress—and being on the JV tennis team together, sharing more math classes, and passing notes in the hallway eventually made us close. So, later, we also started hanging out with Leigh's best friend Laura, who was as unexpectedly sweet as she was intimidating: She was quiet, with mostly black clothing and her reddish hair in an asymmetrical bob, and she was dating a wire-skinny boy in tight jeans who played in a band with the four or five other boys in our school who looked like him. Then we started hanging out with Jess, skinny and eccentric and friends with everybody, and Nola, who said aloud everything you were only supposed to think, among a great number of other things I was pretty sure nobody was even thinking. We sat together at lunch, and we hung out on the weekends. When the movie *Mean Girls* came out in the spring of our junior year, we copied the Plastics and imposed outfit regulations for a week. (On Wednesdays we wore black.) We matched. It was my dream come true.

But my closeness to them felt either very on or very off. And that perceived group closeness usually followed the ups and downs of my friendship with Leigh, who seemed our undeclared leader, though maybe that's something only I believed because I adored her—and feared her. It was never a sure thing. Leigh had this habit of rotating the "best friend" label every few weeks or so and then telling me about it, and I had a bad, embarrassing, and slightly pathetic habit of quietly pressing her whenever I wasn't it. It was more subtle than that sounds, of course—more couched in sixteen-year-old passive aggression: "Laura is really getting on my nerves, but it's like, she's my best friend, so I don't know what to do." "You mean . . . *one* of your best friends?" And so on. I knew I was being needy. But after the first time someone whom you admire (someone with more friends than you, some-one who is taller and more outgoing and better at math than you are) calls you her best friend, and you have not been called anyone's best friend since middle school and we all know that doesn't count, it's hard not to try to trick her into saying it again and again. But then you realize what you actually want is just for her to say it less and mean it more.

Someday late in May we were lying on Leigh's bedroom floor facing one another. I didn't spend a lot of time in there—by the time we became close, Leigh understood that juniors in high school were mostly too old for sleepovers, and I did not. But that day, I had come over after school to give Leigh my year-book because I wanted her to decorate and fill the two pages I'd set aside for her. Girls at my school were always partitioning off parts of their yearbooks for each other. I think it was the one time when being given an assigned spot (or having spots to give) felt really good. Still, some of us were more enthusiastic about it than others. Leigh agreed to sign my pages if I let her hang on to the book for a while, so she'd have enough time. She'd never gotten around to signing my yearbook the year before, and we both felt bad about that—her a bit guilty, me a bit bitter. I needed that spring's yearbook to be different, because I guess I must have felt that a written record of our friendship would make it official. She'd take a few weeks to actually get it back to me (the school year well over by that point), but to her credit, the end result was really lovely.

But on that day, on her floor, things between us were tense. Leigh was talking to me about her boyfriend and about drinking. Both were sore subjects with me.

The topic of alcohol had been easily avoided before the age of sixteen. I only had to think about it in D.A.R.E.: for the week-long unit in fifth grade, for the three-day units in middle school, and for one day each year in high school, when the D.A.R.E. Role Models put white face paint on themselves and on the handful of students they pulled from classes, so that by the end of the day, the number of students walking around school as "ghosts" would, in theory, represent the number of young people who die of drug overdoses each year. Even though it seemed like a pretty slick way to get out of class for a little while, the demonstration never went as smoothly as planned: Usually there were only enough students with white face paint walking around the halls so that every other, non–D.A.R.E. student would see only one the whole day, wonder, "What's going on with that kid?"

and then forget all about it. This was, at least, the way most people reacted.

I, personally, was scared shitless by the entire thing. (Symbolic *dead* people? Walking around in my own *school*?) When the wrecked car of a now-dead drunk driver was installed by D.A.R.E. on our school's front lawn for two days, I averted my eyes as if it were the sun. To look directly at it would have been to acknowledge that this was something I was going to have to deal with—a realization I was putting off, having noticed the hushed (yet proud) cafeteria discussions of prior-weekend debauchery growing and circling in on me. Alcohol was spreading like a liquid virus from the popular kids to the peripherally popular kids to the cool-smart kids, my own friends, and ALL of them were going to die. So when Leigh told me that the weekend before she had had six Mike's Hard Lemonades, looking into her eyes felt like looking into the hollowed eyes of a ghost. A D.A.R.E. ghost.

I was afraid of alcohol, and I was afraid of boys, and I was highly suspicious about the fact that all my friends were starting to spend so much time in their company. And I'm afraid that that made my friends think I was kind of boring to hang out with. I *was* kind of boring to hang out with. At least some of the time. I would have done the exact same things with them every night and weekend if I could: sit on a couch, have a snack, talk, watch *The O.C.*, talk more, never have boys over or look directly at them, but talk about them sometimes, and paint our nails, and be home by curfew. I wanted to *talk* about grown-up stuff. I just didn't feel that it was particularly important for me, or for my friends, to actually *do* any of it. I had only just established a somewhat reliable female social circle. Adding boys—an unstable element—was too stressful to even think about. Maybe in another year, or five. Five years of quiet preparation might actually do it.

The problem with being, as I was then, and on some days continue to be, neither adventurous nor reclusive is that you want friends, but you don't want them to do anything you wouldn't do. But you wouldn't do anything.

It had all been fine, for the most part, until that spring. Leigh had never had a boyfriend, either, and she didn't drink and, as far as I knew (and that was evidently not very far), didn't plan to. She was on student council, a teacher's pet, an excellent student. There were weekend nights when she said she couldn't hang out with me, but I always kind of assumed she was spending most of those nights in, studying alone at home or hanging out with her little brother.

What was really going on, I'd learn that day, was that Leigh was starting to go to parties, where both boys and alcohol (the deadly duo) were present. And no, I was not invited. And yes, a lot of that is probably because I would have disapproved, and because I probably would have said no anyway, because I was scared. And even though I knew that, it still hurt so much. I was being left behind, and that made me angry and sad. I wanted to go with her and I didn't. I definitely didn't want her to know me well enough to know that I would have been too afraid and reserved and rule oriented to go with her. I wanted her either to stand still and then reverse, or to twist my arm into growing up. She didn't.

This is what I was thinking about on her floor, listening to Leigh tell me about her raucous, hard-lemonade-fueled night, and how much fun she'd had there with her new boyfriend,

Andy, who was in the same group as Laura's boyfriend. She was saying she was sorry that she couldn't always hang out when I wanted to, but that "when you get a boyfriend," he becomes the only person you want to spend all your time with. *He* becomes your best friend, and (this part was not said, but was definitively implied) the only friend that really matters. "You'll know what I mean, when you get one," she said.

So that's when I gripped my upper jaw and pulled back the skin and muscle of my face to reveal an alien, like the one in the film *Alien*, and I jumped through the glass in Leigh's window and ate every boyfriend in the city, and the country, and the world. I swallowed them whole, and many of them cried, and those were the ones I liked best.

Because what she said made me mad at Andy, not Leigh. Even though it was her who was sanctimonious and smug, in the same way so many girls I've known have been sanctimonious and smug about their first boyfriends (and their second, and their third . . .), and the things they suddenly see very clearly that we, the hapless single peons, could not possibly understand. Anyway, I guess it's a normal thing to do, even if I hate it every time.

But I didn't really see any of that. I saw a boy inserting himself into my best friend's life and making her act like a crazy person. And this is what I have held against boyfriends all my life: that they are the people who steal your best friends away from you piece by piece, and when they give them back (if they ever do), it is only when they have made your best friends sadder and more heartbroken than when they were first taken. Because that's what it looks like, from here. It had to be his fault, because how could someone who is my best friend ever really choose to see me less and less until we see each other almost not at all? This is what I believed: Best friends, if only by virtue of you calling them your "best friend," just don't *do* that.

But they do.

———

By the time we had started our senior year, Leigh and I were only hanging out every couple of weeks. She was spending more and more of her time with Andy and his group of friends and Laura. Leigh cautiously invited me to one or two of the parties that fall, but I said no. There would be drinking and, worse, there would be couples. I was sure that if I went I would either be arrested, be murdered by my parents, who would snipe me through Leigh's large glass windows, or be a silent and awkward presence, uncomfortably standing alone in corners or hiding in the bathroom (the toilet being the most comforting chair in times of social anxiety). People would ask me if I wanted to drink, and I'd have to say no, because of the parent snipers and because of alcohol poisoning. My friends would talk to me when they weren't making out, but they would be sitting on the laps of their boyfriends, out in the open, and I would not know what to do with my face. I didn't need to have gone to any prior parties to know this was true. I've been to enough since. At every party in the world, there is someone sitting on someone else's lap. People are lap crazy, and it has to be stopped. Has anyone in the history of humankind ever been able to withstand talking to a person who is sitting on another person's lap? Don't you think it's weird to act as though you're maintaining a normal conversation when you're simultaneously perching on another human body?

Anyway. That's not important. (It's kind of important.)

It was at the same time that I was finding my weekends emptier than ever that I started going to my school's basketball games with my friend Jenna—a smart and quietly spunky girl I had known since eighth grade, with whom my on-and-off-again friendship picked back up in senior year thanks to our handful of shared classes and common interests in pirates, Gwen Stefani, and track jackets, among other things—and developed an instantaneously intense and uninformed (because for me, there is no other way) crush on one of our team's stars: a tall, boyish, and freckly point guard named Drew.

No, that's not quite true. I have no idea if he was a point guard. What does a point guard do? Be honest: Doesn't every position in basketball have the same job, when you really think about it?

So it wasn't that I even *liked* basketball. Most sports, to me, are somehow simultaneously boring and impossibly confusing. I'm certainly not good at any of them (see my "Participant's Award" for physical achievement in gym, grades K–8; i.e., the award they give you when you are, at best, still sort of breathing afterward). I always liked baseball best, but I tolerated soccer and basketball—in person only—because there are no helmets and I guess it never hurt anyone to watch a bunch of boys running around in little circles with sweaty hair. It's like I've heard some people say sometimes: "Don't hate the player, hate the game."

But I knew enough to know that our team, that year, was excellent. And my impending graduation—and, with it, the arrival of an incontrovertible slide into adulthood—made me unexpectedly cheery, full of school spirit. I yelled my own graduating class's year and booed at the others (the lowly fresh-men, sophomores, and juniors) loudly at pep fests. I participated in "Spirit Week." And, as with Jake three years earlier, I went crazy for an athlete I knew nothing about. That is why I went to all of the basketball games and stood in the place assigned to people of my social status, like I was supposed to, so that I could watch him.

Even though most of us didn't care about popularity by the end of high school, some of the traditions the ruling class estab-lished early on carried over anyway. It was sort of like the royal family in Great Britain—nobody really understood what made them so special, and we all knew their power was meaningless, but it was like, they'd just been there forever. It would have been more work to uprise than to just let them keep standing in the coolest parts of the hallways or whatever. At the basket-ball games, too; popular boys were always up front, in front of the bleachers, strategically placed for hassling the smaller, less frightening players on the opposing teams. Popular girls stood one row back from that, in the high school's spirit T-shirts with very small shorts, with impeccable hair and makeup. Behind them, the next most popular group of girls and boys—the ath-letic ones, the ones who weren't *quite* good-looking/manipula-tive enough as eleven-year-olds to get in with the first tier when it congealed, sticky and secretive, in the fifth grade, but who were just attractive and wealthy enough to sit comfortably on the second rung of the ladder of High School Glory. These mas-sive groups I never understood. How do groups of twenty-plus people consistently and legitimately enjoy each other's company over the course of fifteen years? And doesn't all the in-group dat-ing make it awkward after a while? I'll never know!

The rest of us, the peons, sat farther back, in an order determined only by how long we spent making ourselves look prettier before showing up. Maybe this seating arrangement was just a result of being trained, having been assigned to our seats from the age of five to the age when we could legally, if we wanted, go to war. Maybe it was all in my head, and if any of my classmates read this they'll be like, "WTF? What a maniac. We just stood wherever there was space when we showed up." To them I'd say: "Whatever. I'm telling my mom you called me that."

So Jenna and I stood about halfway back in the bleachers, and it was there that my slight notice of Drew turned into a full-fledged and hopelessly embarrassing last-ditch attempt at high school romance. I was eighteen and found it intolerable, and frankly a little ridiculous, that I could possibly finish these formative years without having anything, in the high school romance department, to show for it. Wasn't someone supposed to have wedged a love letter through the slats in my locker by then? Wasn't I supposed to have etched my initials, plus a heart, plus another person's initials, into a desk in detention? (Was I supposed to be getting detention?) As I noted in my diary that year: "If someone had told me at the age of 7 that I wouldn't have ANY boyfriends by the age of 18, I would have just given up then." I wrote it as a joke. But I didn't *not* mean it. It never really bothered me that I hadn't had a high school boyfriend until it became almost certain that I couldn't. I couldn't exactly tell what I was missing out on. But it was something.

Watching Drew made this all very clear, and I imagined him stepping in at the last second to serve as my sports-star boyfriend. Here is how it would look: All the girls watching the games would preen and bat their eyes when his jersey number was called in the beginning lineup, but when he was fouled and had to take free throws, he'd bounce the ball twice, kiss his fingers, and point at *me*, as if to say, "I do it all for you." And then everyone in the crowd would look around, trying to pinpoint who the lucky girl was, and they'd see me—and I would kind of be lit from above, like an angel, smiling beatific, supportive, mysterious. After the game, I'd float down the bleachers to where he'd be waiting, sweaty but not gross-sweaty, to hug me and pick me up and kiss me. When we walked outside, he would give me his letter jacket to keep me warm. True, it was not 1955. Boys didn't lend their letter jackets to their girlfriends these days. But he would.

What actually happened after the games was that I'd kind of hang around, making Jenna wait with me, to see if he'd somehow magically know I was hoping to congratulate him for a good performance. By then, I knew him well enough from our shared statistics class—we sat at the same table, which was an exercise in trying to make our knees "accidentally touch"—that it wouldn't have been unreasonable for me to walk up and say hi, but I didn't generally do things like "talk to boys outside of a class-debate context." I wanted him to be the one to want to talk to me. Inevitably, Jenna and I would lurk for about ten minutes, realize that nothing was going to happen, and then walk across the court out to her car to sulk, listen to Ashlee Simpson, and go get ice cream. Then I'd write about how sad it was in my diary. And that made it sadder.

My diary also tells me that there are a handful of things I did in my ill-fated quest to win myself a jock boyfriend and make some culturally recognized meaning of my time in high school, and the main thing that really worries me is that I do not remember doing them *at all*. No, that's not true: The main thing that worries me is the notion that I might not remember, but he does.

One of these small terrors is that I—allegedly, according to the records, which I wrote—made him a Christmas card. The card, apparently, gently suggested that the two of us hang out over winter break, but did not provide him with my phone number. (Embarrassing AND confusing, those main descriptors of everything I've ever done.) I cannot be sure how much glitter was present on the card itself. I don't want to know.

This, unfortunately, is only the third-most-embarrassing thing I did.

Because later I *did* give him my phone number. Not in a normal human way, but in the form of a program in his calculator. This was a relic left over from Squeeze Math (the only thing I still remembered, which I'd have been better off forgetting), in which we'd created and used little programs in our TI-83 calculators for actual math-related purposes, like finding cosines and tangents or whatever. It was also fairly popular, at that time, to have games programmed into our calculators and to borrow them from our friends to see if they had anything new and distracting to share. (I say this because it's true, but also because I want to make myself sound not completely crazy, but I don't think it's going to work.) I am assuming, though I cannot remember for sure, that I "surreptitiously" borrowed Drew's calculator in class one day and wrote a program that contained my phone number. What did I title the program? "Don't Date Me, I Am Clearly Hopeless," presumably. I can't be sure. This memory is untraceable to me.

And finally, the very worst—worse than anything involving a calculator, if you can even believe that.

It was a mistake made on New Year's Eve, the first time I ever learned that's all that is ever really done on that particular night of the year. Jess was invited to a party full of people she wasn't particularly close to, but had been at one time. And because one of those people was Drew, I asked her to extend the invitation to me. I guess I must have figured that it would be a safe enough first teenage party, because the host's mom was going to be there, and therefore there would be no drinking. Boys or alcohol: It had to be either/or, that first time.

What I have to be most thankful for, above all, was that the host, Amy, was friendly and gracious and probably (hopefully) didn't mind that I was there, too—her basement seemed to have more than enough room for one extra weirdo to stand very still by the friend she came with. Movies and dreams led me to believe that if I stood still long enough, Drew would bump into me, and spill punch on me, and then try to clean it off me, and then tell me he thought I was the single most beautiful girl he had ever seen in his many travels across the globe, and then kiss me. Or at least something similar.

Waiting for that to happen was somehow both stressful and boring at the same time. This, I guess, is one of the main reasons why a person like me, then so quiet and watchful, thought it best to avoid going to parties to which she was not directly invited, made up of more people she didn't know than she did, where she would stand near a bunch of admittedly very nice people who were, still, only marginally her friends, to whom she didn't really have anything to talk about, because she would be too busy standing still and worrying about what to do with her arms so that she'd look natural, both alluring and invisible at the same time, if possible: It all just feels like a lot of work. When Jess made me move, we'd walk back and forth from the game area (where people were playing my most-loathed game of all time, Apples to Apples) to the card table set up toward the back, where there were snacks and, most importantly, boys. Including Drew.

What happened next was a blur. I sat down at the table. Jess was somewhere nearby, but my vision clouded her out. There were Tostitos on the table. There was a candle on the table. I said hi to Drew, and started talking to him, but there were also other girls at the table, and I guess I wanted more attention. I picked up a chip, held it in the flame of the candle to see if it would light on fire, and, when it didn't, I put the black and smoky remnant into my mouth, and I swallowed it. I wish I could say that I understood what I was doing. I wish I could say that I was or am secretly a fire-eater, and that after this little fake-out, I pulled out a baton, covered it in gasoline, lit it on fire, and swallowed the flame to rapturous applause. Instead, I just established myself pretty firmly as the weird girl at the party she wasn't invited to who inexplicably tried to light a chip on fire and then ate it.

I know Drew saw it. I know he was intrigued, though I'm fairly sure it was not in the way I intended. He certainly didn't *seem* to suddenly view me as a tough and mysterious vixen with a dark past and a one-way ticket out of this town.

Jess and I left the party just after midnight, after it became clear that nobody (especially not I) was getting kissed. In the few months afterward, I'd keep going to basketball games, up until the very end of the season. I'd keep hoping, with no rationale whatsoever, that Drew would ask me to a dance—first SnoDaze in midwinter, and, when that didn't happen (because why would it have?), with a wishfulness that was much more mild but there all the same, the almighty and glorious Prom in the spring. It wasn't that I really believed he'd be the one to ask me. But I was going to go or I was going to die trying—or both, maybe, dragging my weary and zombified corpse into the banquet hall by my nails, which would have grown curly and long after death, as they do—and that was that.

I had spent my junior and senior years doing Leigh's hair and makeup before each and every formal dance, to all of which she had an automatic in, because such is the good fortune of girls with goddamn, stupid boyfriends. Eventually, especially during that senior spring, these hours were some of the only ones I got to spend alone with her in her house, and it was always a lot of fun right up until the moment she, beautiful and glamorous, left, and I had to get in my car and drive home.

And I just didn't want to have to do that again.

———

For the first seventeen years of my life, I had refused to dance in public. In private, too, really. I wanted no part of it. I went to a school dance in sixth grade, and between the exhaustion that comes from standing in petrified stillness while friends who don't really like you very much sway nearby, and having to watch as four of my grade's prettiest girls began a choreographed dance to the 98 Degrees single "Heat It Up," as a widening, admiring dance circle formed around them, I decided that I'd probably had enough for another five years. Halfway through high school, though, dances started meaning opportunities to wear elaborate gowns and (often ill-conceived) updos. They started meaning that a boy might ask you to do something other than "Pass the stapler" or "Can you move? You are in the way of my locker." High school formals were unquestionably important and grand. They were about true love.

This version of the story, despite everything movies and my delusional teenage heart had encouraged me to hope for, was not my destiny. Drew asked the same girl he'd asked to SnoDaze earlier in the winter, and there were no secretly harbored mutual crushes that wooed me with elaborate displays in the library or the parking lot, either. What is Prom if not a short, springtime, exclusively teenage New Year's Eve? Spent alone or spent in a couple, these nights are never exactly all that you had wished. And usually there is so much more throw-up.

I was not, however, going alone. Two weeks before the dance, my friend Mike—a warm, cute, entertainingly vivacious, and (thinly closeted) gay guy to whom Jenna and I had grown close in the past year—asked me to Prom, and even though I knew he was planning on it beforehand and I had already bought my dress, I was ecstatic. When I got to lunch that day, I found Mike gesturing toward a cardboard Harry Potter–branded treasure chest on the table, in my spot. I opened it and found a scroll with my name written on it in pristine calligraphy. This turned out to be a treasure map, a surprisingly accurate hand drawing of our cafeteria table layout, described in *Mean Girls* fashion, on aged-looking brown paper. Additional scrolls were covered in clues that sent me around the cafeteria, ultimately leading me back to my table, where I found a bouquet of roses on my chair. This is the best way any person has ever been asked to Prom and I don't care to hear any arguments to the contrary.

Five hours before the dance, I went over to Leigh's house to do her hair and makeup as always. She was, of course, going with Andy. She and Laura and their boyfriends were going in a group separate from my own. They'd do pre-game drinking at one of the guys' houses, and then they'd ride in a limo to dinner, and then they'd ride in the limo to Prom. I was jealous of it all: going to Prom with a boyfriend. Drinking (which by then I'd tried once or twice, tentatively, to little fanfare). The limo. These were things I'd imagined my Prom would be. I slicked on her eyeliner, finished curling her hair, and told her she looked great, because she did. I told her I wished I was in her dinner group, because at that moment, I did. And then, because for once I had my own beauty routines to attend to, I left.

My own group's dinner was awkward, and the food was gross. The music the banquet hall DJ played was good, not great. Jenna and her date and Mike and I danced like maniacs, and I didn't care if anybody saw me, because these people and I were almost done spending time together. I saw Drew and his date only once, and it stung only a little. My makeup stayed put and I lost one of my earrings. This is more or less the best a Prom attendee can hope for.

Halfway through the dance, a tipsy, upset-looking Leigh found me in the crowd, and I led her back to the coat check to ask her what was wrong. "Andy," she said. He was being mean, which meant that he was ignoring her, which was something he tended to do when he was drunk. "He won't dance with me," she said. She started to cry, and, feeling sad because she was, and sympathetic toward the injustice of having to cry at Prom, I hugged her. Even though she was never very touchy, she let me.

She and I walked back to the dance floor, where we danced

together, with some of our other friends, for a few songs. I still
have a picture from that part of the night: Our cheeks are very
flushed, and we are both giving the camera a great deal of attitude, her looking downward, her mouth open like it would be
just after saying "Whaaaat!" and me with some sort of duck-
lipped/smile half-breed. We look the way most late-high-school,
early-college-age kids look in pictures they take of one another:
stupid. Stupid, and thrilled to be wherever it is that we are, with
whoever we are with, right at that moment.

Andy and Leigh broke up sometime during the week afterward, for a while. It would take one or two more breakups that
summer for it to really stick. In between their best last days, she
and I would hang out. I felt so close to everybody, and especially to her. (The vague but powerful emotional significance of
having tossed my graduation cap with four hundred other kids
had stuck with me, apparently, for months.) But I would move
for college and so would she, and it would take us four or five
more conversations (drawn out and painful, on the phone, usually while lying on my new dorm room's floor) before I'd realize
that asking her to call me her best friend wasn't going to hold
things together anymore. We knew we would stay connected in
little ways. But as for the day-to-day, for being each other's very
best friend—and as for growing up and going out and leaving
my room for places where other people might be—she knew it
before I did, and accepted it before I did, but still I came to agree
eventually, reluctantly, because I was tired of trailing; college
was the perfect time to start over.

Part Three

♥   ♥   ♥

COLLEGE

Firsts

I T TOOK ME EXACTLY TWO DAYS of college to be caught with my pants around my ankles, but not in the way you're thinking. Not in a good way.

On our second night of school, my new roommate, Joyce, thought it was safe to change from jeans to sweatpants in our room, which was on an all-girls floor, with our door propped open—we were waiting for our new neighbor friends, Colleen and Lacy, to come over to watch *The O.C.* with us—so I decided I did, too. But Joyce is much smaller than I am, and more agile, and maybe those aren't really the reasons it turned out like it did and it was just poor timing, but I do sometimes have trouble managing my limbs efficiently. This is one of the main problems I keep having: I can almost never pull off the things my friends are able to pull off. There is a reason I almost never take risks, and that is because I *know* they will end badly for me. I have no evidence to the contrary.

But I was too thrilled with the new permanent-sleepover feel of my dorm—we had all hit it off so quickly, especially a smaller group of about six of us—to think clearly and self-defensively that night, and so our door was still wide open when my jeans were off and my sweatpants were, at best, around my ankles. And that moment was the same moment when two of our building's cute, male sophomore resident assistants—one of whom I had developed an instant crush on during moving day, when he (because it was his job) helped carry boxes to my room— walked by our door on patrol. I yanked my pants up and kind of tried to jump backward out of view, but obviously it wasn't done quickly enough. My day-old crush, my beloved, stranger RA said, "Whoa, sorry," and averted his eyes, holding out his arm to protect them as though I were a solar eclipse. If this were *Cosmo* magazine, we would have started dating four days later. As it was, we never looked at or spoke to each other ever again.

And that's more or less how I set the tone for my dating life as a college student.

———

That was my wild and crazy second night of college. Rylee's— the actual wild girl across the hall—involved a lot more puking.

It was our third day of orientation and she had apparently gone out to a fraternity party the night before. Already the gossip gears were turning: "Can you believe she had to be carried back by one of the guys from Theta Chi?" "I heard she had, like, eighteen shots." While Joyce and I had stayed in watching TV and either successfully or unsuccessfully changed into sweatpants without being seen, depending on which of us we're talking about, Rylee had gone to a real, genuine, college party. She had a real, bad hangover. Though I had sort of gotten a little drunk with my high school friends a couple of times that previous summer—a half shot of vodka in an entire cup of Fanta—I had never looked the next morning the way Rylee looked now, when a few friends and I stopped by her room to see how she was doing. Cocooned in her bottom bunk, she looked like a mess—pale, stringy hair, dark makeup smudged under her eyes. She looked terrible and cool at the same time. It was hard not to be drawn in by the spectacle of the first girl on our floor to get into something like trouble.

We asked her how she felt and she said, "I'm okay," in a voice much smaller than I expected. She seemed embarrassed by the whole thing. My floormates said they'd stop by again later and walked away, but I hovered for a second. "Do you want to watch a movie or something?" I asked her. She smiled. "Sure." I went back to my room on the other side of the hall and grabbed *A Knight's Tale*, which turns out to be pretty much the best hangover movie ever. It's extremely weird and kind of dumb, and a lot of it doesn't make sense, but there is Heath Ledger, tanned and dirty, and all you have to do is lie there and look at his jawline and hair. He had really great, soothing hair.

I wanted to be Rylee's best friend right away. She was lively and weird. She was curvy but tomboyish, wearing T-shirts and sweatpants almost constantly, without makeup most days, and with her chest-length yellow-blond hair in a messy bun. I don't mean messy bun in an artful, *Vogue*-y way. I mean actually, incredibly messy. She liked Mario Kart and kickball and staying up until 4:00 am talking about philosophy. She mostly seemed to eat just Pizza Lunchables and M&M's. She liked partying and was completely unafraid of interacting with guys, who all seemed to be crazy about her. At the very beginning, we had just two things in common: our sense of humor, and a crush on Aaron.

But I had a crush on him first.

I claimed my territory—as if that's something that can really be done—before she did. I remember it very clearly: "I think that boy is sort of cute," I whispered to her, just yards away from him in the student lounge. She nodded, and looked at him like she was giving him a second thought. "Totally."

In the beginning of the year, our floor of girls and our neighboring floor of boys were so ecstatic to be away from home and around all these hormones that we overlooked a fair amount of personality incompatibility and became a group of twenty people who were all best friends with each other. We ate our meals together, went to frat parties embarrassingly early together, and paired off in insensible couples together. On the same night I got legitimately drunk for the first time—on something called "jungle juice," of course—so did my very tiny pageant-queen-from-the-country friend, who then proceeded to make out with an emo skater boy, date him for two weeks, and break up with him via a two-page handwritten letter slipped under his door.

It was a weird time.

So I may have told Rylee, repeatedly, that I thought Aaron was cute, and I may have flirted with him to whatever minimal extent I could manage, but because we were all in love with each other to some degree, Rylee came to think he was cute, too. And she was going to actually do something about it, which apparently works out better than my preferred method of willing my romantic daydreams to become realities. ("Why does he literally never come to my door, wet from the thunderstorm, to tell me 'It's always been you'?") She started staying up very late with him and his roommate, getting to know them better and playing video games in their room, getting things accomplished well after the hour I decided I needed to go to bed. My hyper-disciplined need to be a functional human during the daytime has always gotten in the way of my nights.

After either five minutes or about a week and a half (I couldn't tell you the difference, it was so quick) of Super Mario Brothers–themed trash-talking, flirting behind shrubbery during our dorm floor's games of capture the flag, and one or two tentative hand-holdings, Rylee and Aaron started "going out." (What is this term? Why do we even use it for anyone under the age of twenty-five anymore? It doesn't describe what is actually done, which in college is sit at library tables together, grind exclusively with one another in frat basements, and make out a lot. Nobody is going anywhere.) I learned of this unpleasant development not from Rylee herself, but from two of our friends who knew of my (yes, uninformed) feelings for Aaron. They were my messengers, and I really did want to shoot them.

I heard a knock on my door and I answered it to find Colleen and Lacy standing there, furrowed eyebrows and heads tilted to the side. They were all simpering with very deliberately sympathetic faces and gestures, but it seemed to me they weren't *not* enjoying being the bearers of bad news. (It's like that a lot, isn't it? It's not about wishing ill on anyone, but rather just enjoying having a task to accomplish. I think.) I hated them for that, but of course, in that moment, I hated Rylee more. "Aaron and Rylee are dating," they were saying. "We are SO sorry." They hugged me cautiously, the way you do when you're simulating what you think good friendship looks like because you're only really a fraction of the way there. When they left, I walked across the hall to the bathroom—the place I always go to deal with feelings like the ones I had then—and cried in a stall, imagining myself as the tragic heroine of an ultimately uplifting romantic comedy. It is always helpful, whenever you have to cry a lot about something, to put the additional pressure of wanting to appear movie-like and desperately, morosely beautiful on yourself.

A little later that afternoon, Rylee came to my room to provide me with a live update of her relationship status. I was sitting on my top bunk bed, which really helped establish the symbolism of me getting on my high horse when she told me what was going on. She knew some vague boundary had been crossed, at least in my mind. She came to my room because she knew I'd be upset, but I don't think she completely understood (or cared) what about this change bothered me. We'd known each other less than a month; what did she owe me, if anything? At the end of our brief conversation, I said to her, "I can see where your priorities are at." She crumpled her face, but it was a hollow gesture and we both knew it. An introductory drama course could have been taught out of my dorm room for all the faux emotion on display that day. Has anyone ever actually been able to guilt-trip a friend into breaking up with her new boyfriend? I don't think that happens, but not for lack of trying.

So I was really, really mad for a few days when Rylee didn't break up with Aaron on the spot, or at least apologize like she meant it. It almost derailed us before we ever got anywhere. It seemed she cared more about dating a boy than she did about building a friendship with me, or with any of the other girls on our floor, and that was everything I'd ever known all over again. I had liked him, too, and still did, and she knew it. And though a sizeable portion of my thoughts might have gone to him in those few weeks, almost none of my actions did. Those were reserved for my new friends, the people I was drawn to instantly.

I wanted to like a boy, but even more than that, I wanted to love these girls. Rylee in particular. So I dropped it, because I was never very good at holding a grudge, and anyway there was nothing left for me to do about it.

But because she was starting a new relationship and doing the things that go with it, and because my friends were finding guys to date or to at least make out with at parties, I started to hear a (imaginary, obviously!) tiny whisper in my ear. It said: Kiss *anybody*.

Kissing someone became very important to me all of a sudden because, technically speaking, I hadn't done it yet. Yes, there had been a fake wedding with a neighborhood friend way back, but even I was not going to try to make that count. Most of the time I didn't really care about the fact that I was eighteen with a pure and celibate mouth, but being around so many girls and boys and knowing how frequently they were touching each other convinced me that freshman year was the time to do something about it. I wanted to get it over with, which is always a good way to ensure that doing it, whatever it is, will fall miles short of your expectations. I did not know this yet. I assumed that my first kiss would be, if not magical, then at least pleasant. How could it not be when everyone around me was so cute? My tiny, central Illinois college had an above-average number of extraordinarily good-looking boys. Tall, too. Well dressed and brilliant, every one.

Of course, hardly any of that was true, but I was living in that glorious early stage of moving somewhere new when you think that you've landed in some treasure trove of beautiful perfect people, before that terrible other stage when you meet most of them and realize you were sorely mistaken. Walking around campus those first few days of my brand-new life was like being a kid in a candy store, if the kid kind of wanted to do inappropriate things with the lollipops.

When I was younger, I had thought that my first kiss would be transformative. I'd always imagined it taking place in the snow, at night, after sledding down a hill with the boy I liked. I was big on imaginary kissing at bottoms of hills. He'd ask me if I'd like to go to the park with him after school, and we'd ice-skate for a little while before finding an old plastic sled near the parking lot. I don't know why it always had to be the case that we *found* it, rather than just brought one along with us. It just seemed more romantic and lucky to leave that part to "chance." So we'd find the sled, and run for the big hill on the other end of the park. He'd sit in the front to protect me from the flying snow, and I'd sit behind him with my arms around his middle. At the bottom we'd tumble off the sled, he'd sort of roll on top of me, and we'd do that romantic comedy thing where two people "fall" on each other and look into each other's eyes and decide that, as long as they're in that position, they might as well fall in love. Then he'd kiss me, and I'd hear fireworks. Then we'd break apart and look up into the sky and there would really *be* fireworks.

The way it actually happened was that I planned a weekend trip to my friend Jess's college in Wisconsin, got drunk, and made out with somebody I didn't particularly like (or...know), and it was gross, and then I never saw him again. So I was only off by a little.

———

When things aren't working out quite the way we Americans have dreamed, we go west, and that, I guess, is what I was doing by taking my make-out mission from Illinois to Wisconsin. (Fine. Northwest.) Things weren't lining up at my own school in that first month and a half, but anything could happen out of state, and it could stay exactly as secret as I wanted it to. Whatever I did in Wisconsin would stay in Wisconsin. It was like traveling across the country for some obscure and minimalist cosmetic surgery. I could get it done and come back looking just slightly different, and people would notice, but they wouldn't be quite sure why. I expected to return to campus a changed woman: wiser, more mature, glowing. Women who do sexual stuff are always glowing.

On the Friday night I got to Jess's dorm, she and her friends and I piled into her tiny room to pre-game and play Circle of Death, which is a game that confuses me as I've never met a person who really enjoys it, but we all played it all the time anyway. Though the anxiety associated with trying to make any given night into THE night was building with every moment, everything was mostly normal until Will, aka one of the *Lisa Frank boyfriends from my youth*, showed up to join us. I was like, "What is this, some Ebeneezer Scrooge/Ghosts of Fake Boyfriends Past situation?" I said that inside of my head, though. To Will I just said, "You're…you, right? From elementary school? Oh my *God*, crazy, how have you been in the last…ten years?" Apparently he just grew up and went to college and had his own life outside the pages of my diary. He was still sweet and still cute. I didn't consider him a potential first kiss, though—he was one of those boys who perpetually blush and was thus far too innocent. Also, it would have probably brought up a lot of unnecessary emotional baggage from the second grade. But his appearance felt momentous nonetheless: Here I was trying to arrange my first-ever adult liaison, and one of my first childhood loves had shown up to give me his (unspoken) blessing. My own redheaded guardian angel of kissing.

I met the perfect candidate soon after, at an apartment party that I followed Jess and her other friends to. His name was Eric and he was Jess's friend from class. "He's kind of a dog," she had warned me earlier, while going through her brain's Rolodex of prospective make-out partners. This is only a problem for a boy you're hoping to date. It's pretty much perfect for a boy you're hoping to furiously make out with for two minutes, tops.

Eric was cute—not my type, but cute. He was blond and tall-ish and frat boy–looking—you know, like, *thick*. Sturdy. He was also very charming. We probably didn't talk about much of anything, but whatever it was *seemed* really amazing during the parts where he was brushing hair off my face. I approved of that wholeheartedly. Angrily moving my own hair off to the side all those years had been a big mistake. When someone else did it, it felt like little birds carrying your hair away in their little feet. It felt like Cinderella. (Fine, I was drunk.) Since my main flirting tactics are to a) make fun of the person and b) run away if you feel like he's looking at you too much, I have no idea what I was doing aside from sneakily shaking my hair back into my face. I thought I was being pretty clear about my intentions, but I am always wrong about everything. Eric left the party after about half an hour.

I asked Jess to explain to me what happened, and she said she'd give Eric a call to see what he was up to then. It turned out that he had gone to another apartment in the building to get drunker and higher. He asked Jess to put me on the phone. I was pretty drunk by that point, too, so I was all grabby for the phone anyway. "Let me talk to him," I said, with more authority than was reasonable. I didn't know him at ALL, but that seemed unimportant. We don't need to go into what was said, but I know that I committed one of the gravest of alcohol-induced sins, which is to yell and slur your words at the same time. I asked him where he went and why he wasn't there any longer and he, flirting under the influence, gently reprimanded me for seeming "not all that interested" when he *was* at the party with me. I told him to come back. I was getting my "first kiss" over and done with if it was the last goddamn thing I ever did.

It was all very touching.

While we waited, Jess and I and a few of her other friends went to lie about in the hallway, to escape the overwhelming heat of too many partiers in too small a space. I was sitting against a wall with my knees pulled up to my chest when Eric showed up looking a little worse for the additional consumption, but still cute. He said hi, and I said hi, and then he put his hands out for my hands and pulled me up off the ground, which was about all the convincing I needed. Sometimes it's really nice to just be picked up.

We went back into the party and Eric and I smushed (not in the *Jersey Shore* sense) against a wall by the door. He put his arms around my waist and just kind of looked at me expectantly. I didn't know why *I* had to be the one to take action, and I was a little too aware of the dozens of people surrounding us in the very well lit apartment. But we looked at each other again, and finally just sort of mashed our faces together. It was about as hot as that sounds, which is to say, it wasn't hot. It was a little bit awful.

What do I remember? My mouth feeling like it was too full

of tongue. My tongue protesting, "I thought we had an arrange-ment, I was perfectly fine in here by myself, I don't know what's happening or who this is in here with me but I'm not too fond of this and I am a little numb anyway and honestly I'd just rather be going to bed." I remember cameras flashing (!!) and squeez-ing my eyes closed tighter, willing them to stop. (Are those pic-tures out there, somewhere? Mail them to me. No, burn them. No, mail them to me.) I remember thinking, "How long must I keep going with this? Will there be a clear signal when it is time to stop? Can I breathe? Am I breathing right now?"

It probably lasted all of a minute or two, which was about a minute or two too long. When it was over we both kind of looked at each other and laughed, and I scurried away to find Jess and apply first aid ChapStick, and that was that. He and I waved good-bye when Jess and I left the party, but neither of us had anything left to say. (What do other/normal people talk about right after they kiss? I have yet to figure this out.) Ours was a brief and joyless affair. It was purely utilitarian and very spitty. I don't think either of us can really be blamed for how disastrously bad it was (though later rendezvous would lead me to believe that maybe I could blame him a little bit, just for the vigorous tongue usage). It was much worse than my expecta-tions, but I also knew that my expectations were pretty much bullshit. At the very least, I had done what I had come there to do: I got my first kiss done and over with.

I felt exactly the same after as I did before, and that's the only part that made me feel bad: that I had let this small and quiet pressure (from nowhere I could even definitively place) get to me, and make me think that there was some need to rush or feel bad about what I had not yet done. It gives the "first" label so much more credit than it is due. When Jess and I would recount the story to our other high school friends over winter break, a few months later, Leigh would tease me about having had my "special first kiss," in a way that felt infantilizing and mean. "You're one of us now, sort of," is how it sounded. "But you *barely* made it." She'd never say it directly. Nobody (or almost nobody) would, because I don't think that anyone thinks they believe that hookups, of whatever base, or relationships with guys can be measured like defining achievements. But you know what? The number of people that do—despite what they say— is so much higher than I ever realized. That's both the worst and the most important thing I learned my entire freshman year of college.

And I didn't—I *don't*—want to be like that. So I stopped rushing. And I went back to my own school for the spring semester, with my own new weird and uncomfortable and funny make-out story to contribute whenever the topic arose in the cafeteria. That part I did love: having something specific and adult-like to share with my new friends. But racing out and around campus to rack up hookups (without really wanting them) just to have something to talk to my friends about? That's just plain lack of creativity.

All's Fair in Love and War

EVEN THOUGH MY INTEREST IN Aaron was uninformed, base-less, hopeless, and lukewarm at the hottest, I still didn't get over it right away. But I did get over it much closer to right away than I'm normally capable of. It was easier than usual because, from the moment he started dating Rylee, he got grosser every day.

One moral of this story is that sometimes, in very specific cases like these, it's actually good when your friend starts dating someone you like even though you wanted to date him yourself, because then she, and not you, will be the one who has to deal with the showerlessness, the Tetris-dependency issues, the per-petual and seemingly permanent wearing of dirty sweatpants, the flirting with other girls, and the general incompatibility that comes along with most relationships between nineteen-year-olds. You get to learn about the person you thought you *really cared about* over an ensuing period of six months, and watch with fascination and mild horror as you are provided with more and more evidence that you actually have not a single fuck-ing clue what you are talking about when you think you like somebody. You get to be there for your friend and help her through problems you are so relieved aren't your own.

Bad relationships and subsequent breakups, if they aren't good for anything else, are useful tools for finding out what friends you like best. Advice and support are hard things to give. It can be a particularly difficult thing to do when you know (or not "know," but *strongly believe with good reason*) your good friend's relationship is going nowhere, but she continues to believe she and her boyfriend are soul mates anyway, even though she cries at least three times a week about something he's done. It's also hard when you don't give a shit about other people's problems. That is not the case for *me*, but it was certainly true for some of our friends when Rylee was going through the pre- and post-breakup stages of her relationship with Aaron.

Something that is very hard to learn and accept about real life is that a lot of people, a surprising number of people, don't really care about anyone but themselves. They pretend to care, and they can go through the motions a little bit for a little while, but when real and sad things happen that last longer than a few days, they lose interest fast. It is best to not have these people be your best friends, because they are terrible. Unfortunately, they are everywhere, and, to make things worse, they sometimes procreate.

Rylee's breakup with Aaron brought her and me closer together because I genuinely cared about her. I'm not trying to be self-righteous about this, but I am literally the best friend a person could ask for and I am a good listener and anybody who doesn't want to be my friend should take a long, hard look at him/herself and whisper, "What is *wrong* with me? Why was I born without the capacity to love?"

When Rylee and Aaron broke up, it happened like this: She did that thing that some other girls I've known do where they suggest that they and their boyfriends (or girlfriends, as I am sure some gay girls do this, too) break up, even though what they want isn't actually to break up, but just to be begged to stay. This, by the way, is another of those things that never works. Aaron said, "Fine, if that's what you want," and Rylee was like, "Actually, wait…haha AHHHH I was just kidding!!!!!!!! I WAS KIDDING, PLEASE. PLEASE." And Aaron said (something like), "Too late. Please excuse me, eight hours of Super Smash Bros. and Cheetos are calling my name."

Then Rylee cried a lot and we did some of the things that you do when you're in college and trying to get over some dumb kid. We had tequila shots (which we somehow used to be able to do without vomiting? I don't know, I'm old now) and danced to the Pussycat Dolls. We watched *When Harry Met Sally* approximately eighty-seven times. She cried every day and I stroked her hair. We got Sad Food from the cafeteria (french fries, Tater Tots, soft-serve ice cream with every topping, chocolate milk). We went to the library not to study, but to mope. We became best friends. We were kindred spirits, Anne of Green Gables and Diana Barry.

And then a few months later, long after she was all better, things got really good.

One day after class I opened my email to find a message from Aaron, and the main reason I knew it was going to be fantastic is because there was a PowerPoint presentation attached. The body of the email informed me that Aaron had put together the presentation for Rylee in the hopes of getting her back, and was sending it to me first for…proofreading, I guess? (Going forward, a mandate: If you're unsure as to the contents of a love letter you're intending to send, be it actual letter, email, PowerPoint presentation, Excel spreadsheet, bar graph, or pie chart, you are almost certainly better off just not sending that letter at all than you are showing it to a single other human being.) The other reason Aaron sent me this perplexing email was, he said, because he also wanted my opinion as to whether or not I thought he "had a shot" at getting Rylee back.

I knew he did not have a shot before I opened the presentation for several reasons, not the least of which was that he was trying to win her back with a PowerPoint presentation. For one, he had started dating another girl immediately, within days, after breaking up with Rylee. Rylee had gone to knock on his door to talk to him, and he said, "Come in," and he and this other girl—whom Aaron had frequently told Rylee was "very cool, a good friend," back when they were together and of whom Rylee had always been suspicious—were lying down together over the comforter on his top bunk bed. I was pretty sure she remembered that day with perfect clarity and an attention to detail no number of slide shows could fog over.

Then there was the AIM conversation that took place after Aaron and the other girl had broken up, in which he saw fit to type the following sentence out to Rylee: "One of the reasons I think we were good together is that you are about a 7 out of 10 (maybe 8 on your good days), and I think I'm about the same."

And finally, not solely because of these events but definitely helped along by them, Rylee had spent their months apart realizing how seriously, *seriously* mismatched they were in the first place, regardless of whether they were both "7"s. "He isn't funny to me," she said one day, the first in a series of slow, spoken realizations. "He never made me laugh. He just tickled me a lot." "I feel like you should have noticed this before," I said, because I'm not helpful.

But when somebody sends you a PowerPoint Presentation of Love that is meant for your best friend, with a postscript that says you shouldn't show it to her yet because this person is later going to send it to her himself, and you know that he doesn't have a shot in hell, you obviously are going to open it anyway. And then you're going to show it to your best friend. And to all of your other roommates, and possibly to anyone in the building who hears you screaming.

There are a lot of things wrong with this particular approach to getting your girlfriend to agree to reenter a relationship with you. Probably the biggest problem is that it's a *PowerPoint presentation*. Nobody likes PowerPoint presentations. They are annoying to produce, they're ugly, they are filled with bullet points and bar graphs and pie charts, and they all too often feature words or phrases that slide or materialize onto the screen from nowhere. Nobody cares more about words just because they appear in an unusual way. This is a promise. I could count the number of times that a PowerPoint presentation has made me say, "Aw, I'm feeling sweet and vaguely romantic" on zero hands, because that has literally never happened. Nobody goes through a set of PowerPoint slides and thinks to herself, "I am growing more content and amorous with each passing slide." A person goes through a set of PowerPoint slides and thinks, "How many stories can I jump from and still live? Are my eyeballs supposed to feel like they want to close forever? Why do I even *have* a job? Why is money so important, anyway? I could live off the land. I have always wanted to forage for berries."

This PowerPoint presentation, about ten or fifteen slides long, featured pictures of Aaron and Rylee, or just Aaron, or just Rylee, all of which were captioned with clichéd romantic sayings. So, for example, there would be, like, a picture of the two of them in the dorm lounge, and underneath it would be the phrase, "You never know what you've got until it's gone" in neon pink Comic Sans or something. And the next slide would be a picture of Rylee smiling, accompanied by the phrase, "Never frown, because you never know when someone is falling in love with your smile." I have never gagged so much in one day. (That's what she said?) (Sorry.)

One of the main issues of contention during Rylee and Aaron's relationship was that she could never pinpoint what exactly it was he liked about her. He seemed to like her company, and sometimes he seemed to like making out, but he was never all that receptive to a lot of the things that make Rylee Rylee. So she'd ask him to tell her why he liked her, and he wouldn't be able to explain it. This PowerPoint was just a great big confirmation of what Rylee had already determined and reconciled months ago: Aaron didn't really love *her*. He loved the idea of having a girlfriend, or something. He loved PowerPoints, possibly.

In my extremely weak defense, I was honest-ish with Aaron when I responded to his email, and told him that I really doubted he still had a chance, and that I was sorry, but it was clear that Rylee had moved on. He emailed her anyway, to ask her if he could show her the presentation. She said no, that there was no chance she was getting back together with him, and nothing would change that. Then he begged her to just watch it, since he had "taken the time" to make it. So she said fine, and he came over and played her the presentation in our basement living room. Only the TV we had down there was very old and the presentation didn't format correctly, so that when it played, all the quotes were clipped from the screen. Of course, Rylee knew what they would have said. But she couldn't admit as much. So she sat through ten minutes of pictures of her and her ex-boyfriend, while that ex-boyfriend muttered angrily about how much better it would be if it were working properly. And somehow, throughout the whole thing, she didn't even laugh once. I think she was in shock. She might still be.

There is probably some lesson in all of this beyond "PowerPoint presentations are the absolute worst." I think one of them is that a woman's friends who are also women are, or at least can be, the most indispensable source of joy and comfort and misery-loving, french fry–eating company in the entire world, and that sometimes it takes a shitty relationship to make a person appreciate that. Another lesson might be that shitty relationships make people cry more than they should and laugh more than is ethically responsible. For instance, I don't always feel great about taping pathetically earnest love letters from my friends' asshole ex-boyfriends to my refrigerator and sometimes performing dramatic readings of them to my party guests. But also: When somebody hurts someone you love very much, how else do you keep going? It has to be made into a joke. "All's fair in love and war."

Actually, that quote might have been in the PowerPoint, too, now that I'm thinking about it.

Trust Issues

ETHAN AND I GOT OFF on the wrong foot at first. Early on in freshman year, before I knew any one person better than anyone else, I remember sitting in the cafeteria at our floor's usual table and hearing him tell one of our friends he was from Hawaii. Because we were square in the middle of Illinois and because I was being sort of an asshole, I said, *"Hawaii? Really. Where are you really from?"* He glared down the table at me. *"Hawaii."* In the beginning of our freshman year, Ethan dressed like a skater, with a backward baseball cap and black earrings that looked like gauges but weren't. The accessories, plus the fact that he was the only person in our group from a place with a coast, made him seem like a much harder kid than he actually was. I didn't see the two of us getting along, but I was mistaken.

Over the course of eating nearly every meal together and spending both nights of every weekend going to the same parties, I decided that Ethan was the funniest person I knew. After our still-massive group came back from going out to the frat parties at night (the only places we had to go), we ran to our rooms to change into sweatpants and grab food to bring with us to the lounge, where we piled all over the floor and furniture, being drunk with one another until three or four in the morning. Ethan would pretty frequently do this not-all-that-accurate but somehow impossibly funny impression of Creed's "With Arms Wide Open," during which he'd close his eyes and growl and reach his arms up toward the ceiling, and I laughed so hard I thought I'd throw up.

Then there were the occasional prank calls to grocery stores and movie theaters. Ethan called the Kroger grocery three blocks from our school and asked if the store clerk knew if they sold "the cereal with the kids on the front of the box." He never said the brand name, or provided any other additional clarifying details. Instead, he just launched into these insanely detailed and inventive descriptions of what the kids on the front of the box were doing. These calls usually lasted about three minutes before the teenage kid on the other end gave up and hung up on him. When he called the local movie theaters, Ethan asked when *Mission Impossible 2* was scheduled to come out. When the employee tried to inform Ethan that that particular movie had come out some time ago, he'd describe the plot of *Mission Impossible*, followed by what he imagined might take place in the sequel. "It looks really good, I really want to know when it's coming out!" he'd say. Rylee and Colleen and I lay in fits on the floor behind him.

When we were *really* bored, on just one or two separate afternoons, a few of us would get in Ethan's car with a globe and a box of macaroni and cheese and drive around our college's small town so that he could confuse unsuspecting strangers. Sometimes he'd pull over to the side of a road and ask someone for directions to the mall, rolling down the window to hand over the globe. A surprising number of people neither laughed nor swore at him, and tried desperately to be kind and helpful. I loved those people very much. When Ethan handed people the box of macaroni instead, those people were usually unamused. Sometimes we'd drive up behind a man (of any age) and Ethan would yell out the window, "Dad? Dad? Dad? DAD!!!" until the man turned around and he'd yell, "Oh, sorry!! I thought you were my father." For reasons I'm sure had a lot to do with the novelty of my being involved with anything remotely prank-like, it was *so* funny.

Though Ethan and I hung out all the time, so did everyone else on our floor. I guess I must have had some form of crush on him, but it was in that friend-like way in which you're hanging out with someone of the sex you usually draw crushes from, and that person is someone who is funny and smart and cute, and there's nothing really off, exactly, but it's not necessarily *on*, either. I think almost all of us felt this way about him. My affection for him grew increasingly romantic-seeming in direct proportion to how many drinks I had consumed and would subside on the mornings and days after, when I remembered that, for all the great things about him, it just didn't feel like something more than friendship.

That was not how Ethan felt.

On an otherwise unremarkable night in January, my friends and I were drinking and standing around at Ethan's new frat house. Because it was one of the nights they made punch, intimate confessions were flowing left and right and, as per usual, it being after 11:00 pm, I had accidentally grown territorial. "I don't like that Ethan's talking to that GIRL," I said to Lacy. "What is her FACE, even." Lacy must have seemed like a worthy confidante that evening (perhaps because she was extremely short, the perfect size for a small and seemingly trustworthy container of secrets), because after we got back to the dorms that night, she ran into my room and told me that Ethan told her that he liked me. "A *lot*, he said!!!" she squealed. I was like, "What?" So she said it again, and I was like, "But what did he say? Are you sure you heard him correctly?" And she told me again, and there was only so much ambiguity you could read into a sentence like "I really like Katie," so I guessed that, even though it made no sense whatsoever, it had to be true.

By then I had spent nineteen years liking people and hoping they might like me back and being used to the fact that they didn't. That was the pattern: Like someone from a distance, close that distance in the smallest way possible, realize nothing good is happening, feel briefly defeated, see someone hot, move on. If I thought it extremely unlikely that the people I held disastrously long and unproductive crushes on might ever reciprocate my moony feelings, I thought it impossible that anyone else could just start liking me of his own accord. I *still* think that sounds impossible. And it's not because I think I'm horrible, because I don't. It's just not how it works.

Boys had always been something that lived only in my head. And I forgot they were real.

That sounds bad. What I mean is that I forgot boys and I could have anything to do with each other. Actually, it's even worse than that. I forgot my dating life could have anything to do with *me*, too. If you only ever like people you don't know and who don't know you, the ball is perpetually in their court. Only they don't realize that you think they're playing basketball with you. They are not actually at the court. You think *you're* there. But really you're not there, either.

Without realizing it, I'd been treating my school crushes like a crush I'd have on a celebrity: You can certainly *hope* that Ryan Gosling will one day accidentally trip you, and then pick you up as you are flying through the air, and hold you above his head the way he did to Emma Stone. And some nights your brain might hold a full conversation with him while you're falling asleep, and it might sound so *natural* that you're sure he must at least have an idea you exist. But still, you're not counting on it, and you're not going to do anything to try to make it happen, because you know that it just won't. Your crush on him—and we are talking about you, here—wouldn't really have anything to do with him, and it wouldn't have anything to do with you. Neither of you knows anything about the other.

That's how all my crushes went: no real boys, no real me. And now that I was thinking about it, that sort of sounded like a problem, or at least an unsustainable model going forward. Pretty much the two most basic components of a realistic dating life were missing.

When I found out that Ethan liked me, I knew that that purely innocent and dreamy part of my life was (well, for the most part) over. And I thought that was pretty scary, and, frankly, a little stupid.

I don't know if this is how you're supposed to feel when someone you like (anyone you like at least somewhat, anyone who is your single, normal, pleasant friend) makes it known that he likes you, but I felt like I had been punched in the stomach and squeezed around the lungs and pinched in the heart valves. I was shocked, afraid, and kind of irritated. That last feeling was hard to explain, but I think it's because I had no warning that he felt that way, no time to prepare or adjust or, most likely, flee in every way possible. It was out of my hands: He liked me, and there was nothing I could do to stop it.

I was, for the first time ever, going to have to make some sort of executive decision, and that's how I learned that executive decisions associated with boys make me seasick.

The next day, Lacy came by my room. She knocked, opened the door when I said "Come in," and, once she saw I was inside, promptly left. This was somewhat suspicious, I thought. It was starting. Before I could decide what to do next (my room was on the sixth floor of our building, and the ceiling tiles appeared firmly glued in place), I heard another knock on my door. I answered it to find Ethan, who I reluctantly allowed in. He sat on my floor and I sat back at my desk chair. He appeared to be having a hard time remembering to breathe. His nervousness was so severely apparent that I couldn't help but laugh.

"What???" he said, panicking.

"Nothing. What's up?" I said. I was terrified, too. Luckily, the fear kind of petrified me into place, so I knew I couldn't get up and leave right then.

"Well I don't know if Lacy told you, but I told her last night that I like you. And...well, I was going to say I've liked you for like a million years, but that would obviously be an exaggeration. But basically for a million years. And there's a concert in February and I'm wondering if you'll go with me. But since that's a ways away, maybe we could do something else sooner," he said. Then he breathed again.

It was very sweet and adorable.

At first I said yes, sort of, because I panicked and couldn't think of a good reason to say no—I said maybe to the concert, and that I was agreeable to "seeing how things go"—but a day later, I called him back into my dorm room and told him I couldn't go with him. I told him that I just wanted to be friends, and that I didn't want things to be "weird" for our whole group. (Maintenance of peaceful group relations is VERY important to us authoritative single people. It's because we care, and maybe just a little because we're afraid of uncontrollable events.) I meant what I said in as much as I had no idea what I was talking about, but felt some vague certainty that any kind of change would be a bad thing. I thought I probably liked him at least a little, but I also wasn't sure. There was nothing familiarly crush-like in the way I felt about him: no butterflies, no daydreams, no emptily premised attempts to see him or talk to him. Plus, though I obviously enjoyed the idea of a boyfriend as some vague and theoretical concept that kissed me beneath weather elements, I found this unexpectedly genuine possibility—the sudden and physical reality—of having one absurd. What would we even *do*?

At first, my friends were only modestly in favor and understanding of my response. They knew how well we got along, and had seen the way I'd grow increasingly affectionate toward and protective of him on weekend nights. They were also aware that my dating history was, at best, imaginary. They told me that dating him wouldn't hurt, and that maybe part of the reason I was saying no was because I was scared. Neither of these things, by the way, is mutually exclusive from making a correct and appropriate decision not to do something. Everyone acts like they are, but they aren't. Both of these sentiments have informed my decision not to skydive, for example. Yes, I could be (relatively) sure that I would be fine. But was mere survival really enough?

So I spent a lot of time talking to my friends about feeling unsure about my decision, and they talked to me about why I thought I felt unsure and whether I was sure I was unsure, and that made me even more unsure. I was sure of it.

And then I did too much thinking for a few months.

While that was going on, for the rest of the semester, Ethan kept liking me and I kept trying to figure out whether or not I liked him back. We sometimes drunkenly held hands at parties, even though I was sometimes weirded out by how much longer my fingers were than his, and I tried to tell the difference between the mild thrill associated with doing something cute and physical with *any* nice boy, and whatever I felt doing it with this one. We got mildly jealous of each other whenever the other talked to boys or girls, and we whispered about that to our friends, who all told each other and then us. And once or twice, we tried to passive-aggressively constrain each other's decisions about party behavior, though neither of us really had the right. Okay, fine. That was mostly me.

We were at his frat house one night when I saw him hand cash to another guy there, take a little envelope in return, and place it in his pocket. I strode over to him like a crazed person full of one million cups of punch and said, "WHAT is in your POCKET??" He knew my feelings about drugs—that I was against them, supposedly, although I was and continue to be quietly and magnetically drawn to the people who use the milder variants—so he just looked at me, guilty. I reached into his front pocket and pulled out the tiniest clear envelope filled one-quarter full with the tiniest portion of marijuana ever known to man. Still, I had never even seen it before, so for all I knew this was practically an ounce. Thirty years in jail, minimum.

I closed my fist around the packet and ran around the corner into the bathroom. Ethan followed. I shut the door behind him.

"I'm flushing this!" I said, holding my clenched hand over the toilet.

"Fine," he said.

"Wait, what?" I said. I hadn't really been planning for what would happen next, but experience and world knowledge led me to believe that stealing people's purchased possessions generally led to a more dramatic argument. "You spent money on this. How much was this?"

"Ten dollars," he said. "But I'd rather lose it than have you be mad at me."

I wanted to do it. I thought about doing it. I hadn't expected this to go over so smoothly. It was just too easy, and I felt just a little bit too bad, so I handed the pouch back.

"Just take it," I said.

He did. And then he walked over to the toilet and flushed it down himself.

A true fact that is kind of sad, maybe: This is THE most romantic thing that has ever happened to me, and it involves both drugs and a toilet. In a movie (or perhaps in some lame D.A.R.E. PSA aimed toward hormonal teenagers) I would have rewarded him by slamming him against the door and making out with him. But I didn't do that. I smiled and I fled the scene.

Here is a quandary: When you possess some charged and flighty need to extricate yourself from potentially romantic situations both with boys you like and, separately, boys who like you, how do you tell the difference between them? How can you tell if someone is both?

That was my main problem all semester, trying to decide whether I liked him, or whether I was just all too aware of the fact that he, the first of his kind, liked me. I thought about it from every angle I could think of, and I tried to pinpoint what exactly about him made me NOT want to date him, and when I could think of nothing specific I asked my friends for their help. "Do YOU think I like him?" I asked them, every couple of days, for a length of time that was likely embarrassing. This was the first time I'd ever been in the position to hand over my boy-related decisions to my friends—being as it was the first time I had some real decision to make—and right away I understood why so many of us do this to each other all the time: It is addictive and soothing. "Do YOU think we should break up?" "Do YOU think I'm being needy because I'm afraid of losing him?" The idea that somebody else could know you better than you is always so very insulting up until the point that it's comforting and easy. I am sick of dealing with my life. YOU take it, for once.

And maybe it seems like it shouldn't have been something to agonize and hand-wring over. But I didn't know that yet. This was the weirdest thing that had ever happened to me. And I didn't yet know that I could be trusted with myself—that simply not wanting to do something could be reason enough not to do it. I thought that if I didn't want to date him, and if I hadn't dated anyone previously, I might be doing something wrong.

One night in April, my last night at school before heading home for a week prior to a May term school trip to China, we were together at Ethan's frat house. It was not a weekend night so there weren't many people there, but my friends and I were saying our end-of-year good-byes and drinking some very terrible peach schnapps. Ethan and I leaned against the piano in the dining room area and he told me he still liked me a lot. He told me that he wanted to kiss me, but that he wouldn't want "our first kiss" to be when we were drunk. And I guess I must have figured that it wasn't going to happen any other way, and maybe that's what made me say, "You can kiss me if you want." So he did. And it was much nicer than the time I kissed Eric, six months earlier. But to some extent it was drunk kissing all the same. Every similar scenario to come, with boys I didn't know yet, would be like that, too. Yogurt and drunk kissing—these are things that I, as a woman, feel I should be enjoying more. Alas, it is not so. They're both fine, I guess, but I'm also pretty sure better experiences exist.

The next day I left. I said good-bye to everyone, including Ethan, and neither of us brought it up. There was no big "talk" had. It didn't seem like he wanted to. I *knew* I didn't want to. I didn't have any idea what to say.

Thinking about it later—cheesily and melodramatically, looking at the rolling hillsides of rural China through a bus window and picturing myself, of course, as the star of a melancholy movie—would give me slight and brief heart palpitations, though I was certain (or pretty certain) that had more to do with the objective sweetness of it all than pining for some grand romantic opportunity I'd denied myself. Sometimes, over the summer, I'd feel almost guilty, like I was doing myself a disservice by not "taking a chance" on something that scared me. I didn't want to be not dating someone just because I was used to not dating anyone. But, on the other hand, one of the nice things about being single all the time is that there's no built-up generalized desire for romantic companionship to factor into the decision. I have no impulse to date just to date. When people say, "Ugh, I have a date tonight. I am not looking forward to it," I am incapable of understanding that as a statement. And when I say I'm pretty sure I don't like someone enough to date him, but I admit, when pressed, that I don't know how to be *sure*, and then the people around me take that as incontrovertible evidence that I should proceed anyway—I don't understand that, either. Everyone means so well, but how weird is it that so many girls spend so much time convincing each other to date people we aren't sure we want to date? What are we pushing each other toward? Look, I'm literally as little of an expert as you can be at something when it comes to dating. I just don't get any of this.

Still, it's me who has to decide in the end, however much I wish that weren't the case, however much I wish I had a clone like the littlest Lawrence brother in that Disney movie, just for handling areas like these. I have to trust myself when I think someone is better off as my friend. I have to trust myself to know when these things that don't make sense to anyone else—the way they didn't back then, when all our friends thought we'd be perfect—*do* make sense to me. When I know, I will know. I think.

There were times, a year or so later, when I'd doubt myself. I'd wonder about Ethan and me, especially when we were separated by states and oceans, and especially when I'd listen to some song off of one of the mixes he'd made for me during our freshman year. (I know, ugh.) But I was missing feelings that weren't quite ever there. I was feeling bad about feeling unsure when everything on paper said I should have been in love.

The problem is that paper just isn't all that trustworthy. You can write basically anything on it. I don't even know why that's a saying.

Here is what I was starting to trust: me. Not even because I was always right, though I promise you, I swear, that I have always come incredibly, almost-suspiciously-close-to-perfectly close. Nor is it even because other people were ever really and totally wrong. Most people's advice is meant, with care and caution, to steer you toward some positive unknown. Most people assume that when you talk for forty days and forty nights about a guy it's because you DO want to date him, and that your maybe is closest to an almost-yes. They will think that you are uncertain if you say you are. But at some point you'll make up your mind, even if it's more because you have to than because you are absolutely certain you could never wonder about having chosen something else. Either way, I think it will be more okay than not. You can talk for several hundred hours to figure that out, too. And eventually, after your voice is no longer working and you've finally exhausted not only everyone around you but yourself, you tell your friends you think you might have known what to do all along. They will say, "Oh. Well, let's go out, then," and you will. And everything will be fine.

Never Have I Ever

SOMEBODY SHOULD BE MONITORING MORE carefully the decisions of people who are crazy for each other. Because before
sophomore year started, my group of friends and I—having
whittled ourselves down to a tight, seemingly indestructible
five—made the adorable and unwise decision to live together
in one room for the entire coming year, and someone should
have stopped us. It was just one room. One room with two bunk
beds and one loft. I had never been to sleepaway camp as a kid
because I had been too scared to leave home, and I imagined
that sharing a room with my four best friends would make up
for that. We'd play Truth or Dare every night. We'd lie in our
beds and laugh until six in the morning. We might even play
that game where you try to make each other levitate, whispering
"light as a feather, stiff as a board," and we would say we didn't
believe it would work, but we all kind of would.

This is not how things generally turn out when five nineteen-
year-old women live in a room together, no matter how big it
might be. It's like that, a little, at first. On an early fall weekend,
we sat in a circle in the middle of the floor and played a round of
Never Have I Ever, that great simultaneous divider and unifier of

college girls. There is always a fork in the road, a wild divergence in the earliest quarter of the game, and if you do not have some baseline of sexual achievement, the rest of the game becomes very boring very quickly. I could have left the room and my inability to participate would have been no more noticed than it was with me there. I could have left the state. I kind of wanted to. Whereas Rylee's fingers disappeared into her fist within minutes, mine remained stretched out and self-conscious about even being attached to my hand, which never did anything dramatic or stupid or cool. People usually pretend to be embarrassed when they play (and win) Never Have I Ever, but this is a game that is fundamentally about bragging. And according to the way the game was going, I had done nothing worth writing home about. Not that my parents would ever want to receive that kind of letter. But you know what I mean.

Somehow, by the middle of fall in our sophomore year, Rylee had gotten a lot farther down that road than I had realized. She was having sex—not frequently but not infrequently, either, with not all that many guys but with more than zero. (At that point, she stood out: Lacy and Joyce had long-term boyfriends whom they were presumably sleeping with, but they were always both extremely reticent about that topic. Colleen wasn't dating or having sex, but she was making out with impressive vigor.) And even though I always knew when Rylee's rendezvous were happening, it's sometimes hard to understand the magnitude of one's experiential difference from others until you hear it listed off, in lots of vivid and alarming details, in a game of Never Have I Ever. That first time, it felt kind of bad—funny, but also kind of bad—but I thought it might end up being okay if I could just have some time to catch up. But Rylee was just a much faster runner than most of us, and in sophomore year she really took off. This is not necessarily hard to do when one's opponents are standing motionless. But still.

So over the next couple of months we, the other four, got mad at her. Not just for having sex, though that, I'm afraid, was not a small part. It was because she was sleeping with guys who treated her like shit, ones who refused to walk her home and, occasionally, ones who ended up having girlfriends who were still in high school. It was because she'd always start her partying with us and end it without us, disappearing halfway through most nights to follow guys back to wherever. It was because we were worried. It was because she wasn't using thirty-seven forms of birth control all at once, even though I kept insinuating that would really be her best bet. It was because she was drinking a lot, choosing to do these things to be happy but never seeming all that happy the next day, or the one after that. It was because we were at once self-righteous and jealous—self-righteous because we didn't need that kind of attention, jealous because we sometimes wanted it anyway.

We started fighting, vicariously, through our utilities. I turned up the air conditioner at night, and someone else would sneak over to turn it all the way off at 4:00 am so that I woke up sweaty. Rylee stayed up well past midnight talking to guys on AIM on her desktop computer, and the next morning I would tell her that her keyboard was oppressively loud. Colleen nodded. The late-night instant messaging had to go, we agreed. She really punched those keys. Rylee retaliated by taking baths in the communal bathroom we shared among eight of us on the floor, locking the door and soaking for over an hour. We all shared that big room, it was all of ours, but none of us were really welcome. It was just definitely, definitely too many people in one room.

At the end of the semester, Rylee moved out. Lacy moved with her, and the two of them got a double in another dorm building on campus. It couldn't have been more than a hundred yards away. Still, our respective rooms were much quieter and calmer and we thought it would help. And it did, a little. But it's hard to smooth over a semester's worth of built-up resentment. It's hard to stop a roll once you're on it. Rylee kept distancing herself from us, and somewhere along the way, in late mushy winter, Lacy (who was prone, when she was stressed or bothered by whatever thing, to periods of bitchy, unexplained silence, ignoring the people around her to the point of ridiculousness) inflicted an especially unforgiving silent treatment on her. This made Rylee run farther and faster still, to the point where I could hardly see her any longer.

But things got a bit better between us (at least, between me and Colleen and Rylee) for no good reason other than that we were tired, and it became April. April and September, in the Midwest at least, are the two months that usually make everything a little easier to take. Spring made us all happier, made us miss each other. It made us all want to chase boys with renewed energy, and so it seemed pretty unfair to keep judging Rylee for doing the same, but on a bigger and more successful and sexier scale. It wasn't a perfect reversal, but it was better.

April also marked a full year gone since I had last kissed anyone. It was not for that reason alone that I lost my mind, but it did not hurt. It had been a Cold War year, and I was sick of hearing about everyone else's advancements. I wanted to make out with someone again as soon as possible, and maybe, hopefully, even progress a bit farther than where I'd been, which would not have been hard at all. This is some version of what I said to myself early that spring: To the moon, or bust.

————————

You know that thing people say about sex being like pizza? That even when it's bad, it's good? I have another proposal, another sexual-activity-as-food analogy: Kissing is like a milk shake. I'm going to go at this in a few different ways, so just hang in there. Even when you're starting to feel sick, you want to keep going. Even when your mouth is tired, you want to keep suctioning. It will make you wonder if you even know how your mouth works. You will realize that breathing through your nose has its limits. Something will feel very wrong, and kind of frustrating, but it will also feel very right. You want it always, but especially while on your period.

And it's just kind of hard to leave well enough alone.

It was thanks to Colleen's, Rylee's, and my participation in college tennis that year that we had come into contact with this small yet powerful bastion of male sexuality going by the inauspicious name of Dylan. He was a freshman on the boys' team, and we didn't know anything about him apart from the fact that he was dead sexy. He didn't talk much, but when he did he was funny and charming. He was persistently tanned, with green eyes and a mop of black hair. A hot, well-kept mop. I want to say that he looked vaguely like Adrien Brody, but I'm not even sure that's fair. They both had black hair and they're both sexy in a way that can't really be explained, so I guess there's that. I didn't have a legitimate crush on him or anything—even *I* knew this was someone I could not reasonably hope to date. His existence was one of those rare occasions where everyone gathers around to simply admire someone's beauty, without really feeling the need to compete over it or make it an issue. Our girls' tennis team viewed Dylan as our tiny, small, hot, perfect tennis trophy man. Sure, we'd tease each other—"I got to sit by Dylan in the trainer's office while we both got our ankles wrapped, like soul mates." "Shut up, I hate you, I hope you actually die."—but we knew that Dylan was a precious natural resource, meant to be shared and used only sparingly. He was like sexy coal.

That being said, one hundred percent of us would absolutely have made out (etc.) with him if given the chance. So I wasn't crossing the line when I decided to mine a little bit of Dylan for myself. (Ugh, this coal metaphor!) Any one of us would have done the same thing. Any one of us would have met the same sad fate that I did. It's not about *me*, it's about *nature*. Probably.

I don't know what came over me the night it happened. I've shared my theories, but only with the recognition that they don't quite cover it all. I am not the sort of person who just decides she's going to win somebody over and then does it. I am not a good aggressor. I am not a lighthouse. I'd never before set out on a boy-related mission and actually accomplished it, and I never have since, either. I am sure this was something cosmic, something magical. I think it was the tequila.

As we pre-gamed in Rylee and Lacy's dorm room that night, I told my friends about my plan and they cooed in a way that was somehow both approving and wary. They knew, by the laws of nature, that they could not stop me. But neither could they protect me from whatever might happen next. I saw the fear in their faces, but I ignored it, because I was maniacal by that point. "Mark my words," I told them, without further clarification. "Mark...my...words."

My mission was not elegant. I can admit that now. It involved more running, more drunken yelling, and more semi-hostile interrogation of Dylan's frat brothers than I would have liked. Sure, in a perfect world I would not have called his friend "black shirt guy" quite so many times, or at all. And yes, it probably came off more rude than it did flirtatious when I threw two of Dylan's cigarettes on the ground, once I finally found him in the courtyard behind his frat house. I was a creature possessed. So after just a few moments spent standing alongside Dylan and my friends, I decided to take action. I grabbed his hand and dragged him out to the basement dance floor. I don't know if I even *said* anything. I can't recall, and I don't think that's even (just) because I was drunk. We went to the farthest wall and went about "dancing," which is to say that we swayed in the same directions together at a proximity that might be considered inappropriate in most contexts. At first my back was against his front, but I turned around to face him after a few songs. My leg was sort of in between his legs and my hands were up on the wall behind him. Was I trapping him, a little bit? It might have looked like I was trapping him.

Dylan and I did that look-at-each-other-until-something-happens thing, which is so frustrating I cannot stand it, so I kissed him. I wasn't about to let another Eric situation happen. I wasn't going to let Sexy Coal get away just because I didn't show enough interest when I had the chance. The kissing itself was just all right. Better technique than Eric, more thrilling than Ethan, but does that really mean anything? It was the kind of good kissing that is really only good because of how hot the person you're doing it with is. So we made out for parts of a song, danced a little bit more, made out a little more, and repeated. It's not so much that I was having a genuinely great time as it was that I didn't know when, or how, to stop. I sort of felt like, if I had put in all that work, and actually made this thing happen, and he was willing, I might as well keep kissing him until some third party legitimately forced me to cease and desist.

That happened in a much realer way than I was expecting.

Suddenly, a girl I had never seen before was in my face and screaming at me. She wasn't mad, at first. Just drunk.

"Oh my GOD, my boyfriend just totally yelled at me because he thought that you were ME and that I was making out with some other guy!!!" she squealed.

I was confused for many reasons, among which were the facts that I was at least five inches taller and five shades paler than she was. Nobody with any kind of vision would confuse us in a lineup. But it was sort of a funny thing to have happen, so I laughed in a way that I hoped would suggest that I wanted her to see I was kind of busy at the moment.

"Oh, haha, nope!" I said. *Back slowly away from Sexy Coal*, I thought, *and nobody gets hurt.*

I turned back around, unknowingly leaving a quickly forming wall cloud in my wake. It was happening. I had broken a law of physics or something similar—whatever rule it is that states that perfect hot trophy people are not to be messed with, lest you set the earth's weather systems off balance. Behind me, the girl started screaming. I didn't even actually hear it, because I had tequila earmuffs on (that IS a thing). Later, in the post-apocalyptic world that was born the next day, my friends told me they saw her storm off screaming about "that fucking bitch" she'd just talked to. I would never learn why. My best guess is that she thought I somehow insinuated that we could *never* be mistaken for one another? Like I thought she was uglier than me or something? I really don't know. There is probably no real answer to be had, other than the fact that karma had stepped in to take me down a notch.

That was penance part one.

Part two came later in the night, and it was so much worse. After a few more rounds of making out—my lips starting to hurt, but my liquid brain refusing to just call it a night—Dylan took a pause to tell me he thought it was time he headed back. I could hardly hear the words coming from his mouth, because of the howling desert winds that had taken up spinning around us. This was not how it was supposed to go. He was supposed to want to keep kissing me. He was supposed to ask me to come back to his dorm, so that I could sleep over and then have to walk back in the morning in my shiny party clothes. I (probably) didn't want to have sex with him, but I wanted to do at least one or two semi-gross steps beyond the making out we had already done. I wanted some goddamn progress.

"Are you sure? Really? You're leaving?" I asked, still holding his hand.

"Yeah . . . I've gotta go do some homework."

And just like that, it was quiet. The clock struck midnight—midnight on a *Saturday*—and I turned into a pumpkin.

———

Allow me to take a brief intermission here to explain that there will be no sex. Not with Dylan (which I know might be surprising given how well things were going where we left off, a few sentences ago), and not with any of the guys I haven't introduced you to yet. Not with any secret, lurking strangers I'm keeping hidden in between. It hasn't happened. It's not happening. It's going to happen (I hope??), but it won't be here. Let me just say this: Tina Fey once said, a few years ago, that she was twenty-four when she had sex for the first time because she "couldn't give it away." From what I could gather via the Internet, everyone seemed to think that sounded pretty late. I was twenty-two when she told that story, and I worshipped Tina Fey then as I do now. So I held that deadline out in front of me, on the peripheries of my mind, and I only worried about how old I'd be when it happened until the day I turned twenty-four without it having happened, and then a bit more for a couple of months after that. Then I stopped caring about the hypothetical age I'd be when it happens, because I knew this much: I will definitely be even older than Tina Fey was. Oh well.

Here are the reasons: I mostly haven't had chances, and when I've had chances I haven't realized it. Or I did, but didn't want them. An example: When I was a senior in college my cute friend Johnny, who was drunk and had already, I think, fallen asleep once that night, made out with me on a couch in his house, and then sort of pulled me down so that I was lying on top of him, but backward. Just . . . backward, my back side on his front side, the way two people would look if they had been stacked. He was weird, really, and this sort of move was not unprecedented coming from him, and he was just my friend who liked making out, so I didn't really think anything more about it when, from *below me*, he reached around and slid two fingers—forefinger and middle finger, but wouldn't it be funny if it were the pinkie and the thumb?—down my shirt and one inch deep into my bra. And all I did was lie there. I thought his fingers needed a resting place, maybe. I was tired. After a few minutes, I gently grasped his wrist, lifted his arm, and let it flop to the side of the couch. "Okay," I said. "Good night." Then I went home.

Some time later, my friends would tell me that that was a sign I was supposed to flip over and proceed with . . . doing stuff. "Are you serious?" I said. They nodded. They were all sure of it, somehow. Unanimously so. "I don't understand you people," I said.

I just don't know how anyone ever knows what to do with their bodies. I catch myself worrying about what my arms are doing when I am walking alone, and that is just walking. Alone.

So I am a basket case, generally, and picky, and have almost always had crushes on people who usually don't have crushes on me, and it's rare that I'm so attracted to a stranger that I could imagine having sex with him at that exact moment. And even when that has been true, I am only able to talk about thinking about it, from a safe distance. I have no idea what I'd actually *do* about it. But generally speaking, I'd like to date someone, at least a little, first. Add all this to my somewhat looming height, an unintentional bracing hostility toward people I don't know well, and an end to the era in my life when I might have felt the need to do something the first time to get it over with, and it's not hard to end up a twenty-five-year-old who hasn't had sex. I put practically no effort into it at all. And that's why I don't think we should be calling people "virgins," or implying that virginity is a noun you can lose. These words insinuate a preciousness that I do not feel. My vagina, while nice and useful, is not an orchid.

So if someone around me says something about "virgins" being helpless or hopeless or sad or weak, or I watch someone tell someone else that he would become more relaxed and more fun, happier, and better all around if only he would get *laid*, that is how I know that person is a dummy and I don't want to talk to him or her any longer. Sex is not a wizard, whatever magical-seeming properties it might possess in its better forms. If your friend says to you, "You're being mean, you need to get laid," your problem is not sex. Your problems are that you might be acting like an asshole, and your friends are definitely idiots. I have lived twenty-five years in this body by myself, and I feel pretty confident that, by now, my personality is staying as it is. I'm going to stay a little uptight and anxious. I'm going to continue enjoying plans and Post-its and clean, orderly spaces. And though nobody has been dumb enough to say anything close to "You need to get laid" to my face, I resent the idea that anyone might think, if they knew my history, that I'd be slightly different by virtue of having a penis—however briefly—inside me. That is some phallocentric bullshit if I ever heard any. Hypothetical penises don't make the rules. I make the rules. I love the rules.

And one last small tirade on female sexuality before we drop all this and never speak of it again, before we return to Saturday at midnight: Guys who would make fun of girls for sexual inexperience are terrible people, and when girls do it to other girls it feels even shittier. Guys who shame girls who haven't had sex want them to feel like they aren't doing their job, which is to be sexually available and attractive to guys. (And never mind if they are gay, or just uninterested.) Girls who shame other girls for these reasons are helping those guys. They are saying this:

You are not accomplished where it matters, and I am better than you. I have proven that men find me attractive, and that is what counts. These people, boys and girls and men and women alike, are all dickheads. They make me so mad that I have to move on.

So there will be no sex, and though I really hope it is not always that way, that is fine. Sometimes it's annoying—mostly in the loins region. Loinal region?—and obviously I'm going to get tired of it at certain points more than others, but it's fine. I'm no longer bothered by things I haven't done, simply for not having done them yet. I probably wouldn't have *ever* been bothered, at least not in the timeline sense of it, if movies and TV and a handful of very loud, awful people didn't keep bothering me and the people in my vicinity about it all the time. Jesus Christ!!

But okay, back to Dylan. This whole time, I've just been standing confused in that frat house basement. Homework! Get a load of *that*.

————

There are an amazing number of questions that fly through a person's head when the person she's just made out with tells her that the reason he can no longer make out is that he has to go do homework. At midnight. On a Saturday. The main one is just "What?" Some of the others are "How did I get here, to this place in my life?," "Can someone sweep me out of here with a cane like in the old movies?," and "What am I going to eat when I get home that could help make up for this?"

I suppose I could have said something like "I'll come help you," or "Can I come with?" but that would have required a tenacity I've never had for situations like these. Besides, I was embarrassed enough as it was. I did not need a second no. And even if he hadn't split like that, even if I had asked if I could go wherever it was he was really going, I didn't know what I would have done when I got there. We both knew, I'm assuming, that sex was not really in the cards. We were barely even playing cards. So he walked out. And the next morning, in the cafeteria, I told my friends the full account of what happened, and they laughed. I laughed, too. I had a new war story.

None of this is to say that I gave up hoping we'd get to make out (etc.) again, just once more at least. I was embarrassed, but not THAT embarrassed. Maybe he really HAD gone to do homework? No. I never thought, really and sincerely, that that could be true. But because we were friendly thanks to tennis, and because he hadn't seemed opposed to the making out itself, and because he was so hot, I still hoped to summon that night's power again, because up until, say, 11:55 pm, it had been pretty exhilarating. I had been, in admittedly relative terms, forward with someone I had really wanted to be forward with. For one night—well, for part of one night—I'd been a lighthouse.

———

Rylee, meanwhile, having taken only a very brief break, had resumed getting into trouble, and by then the school had noticed.

It was at the end of a bad week in May—our fighting having picked back up, the spring magic only able to last so long when the same things that made you mad keep happening—when a mutual friend called me around twelve-thirty on a Friday night to tell me that she'd found Rylee on the floor in the girls' bathroom, passed out and ashen. The friend had called for an ambulance and was on the way over to my dorm to pick up one of my roommates and me—already home from a bust of a party, at which I talked to Dylan but did not kiss him even a little—to go to the hospital. We sat in the emergency waiting room for twenty minutes, until a nurse allowed us to see her.

People don't look real lying on hospital beds. They look like dolls, and you sit next to them waiting for the real live version to walk around the corner to sit by you and comfort you. It was scary those first few moments, until she awoke as we walked through the curtain.

"HEY KATIE DID YOU GET TO MAKE OUT WITH DYLAN???" she screamed.

Everyone in the room, including the two nurses handling her IV and various tubes, burst out laughing. Any small moment of relief is funnier than it should be at the hospital. Clearly, Rylee was not in the best shape she had ever been in. But that was still her lying there, charming and vibrant as ever, concerned more with my romantic pursuits that night than with her own sorry state. I loved her for that.

"No, I'm afraid I didn't," I said.

"Oh well," she said, eyes fluttering. "There's . . . will . . . always be . . . the next times."

The nurses enlisted my help in holding a bucket for her to throw up into, which is probably one of those things you can never imagine being willing to do before college. It made me feel better, and less afraid. After a year spent trying to help someone deal with things I didn't understand without having the first idea how to do it, it felt nice to have it be so simple: Hold this bucket, and don't move. She dry-heaved, spitting (or trying to spit) into the bucket I was holding next to her head. "Well

THAT didn't go anywhere but my mouth," she said. I tried not to laugh too much, but it was no use.

She was always going to be excited for me, I realized. It didn't matter to her that she was so far ahead with sex and guys, or that I couldn't commiserate in whatever sex issues people who are having sex have. She was never going to patronize me. She would never tell me that when *I* had sex, or when *I* had a boyfriend, I would understand. I think I had assumed that she would be that way. Her drunken hospital proclamations indicated otherwise, and that made me happy. So that, plus the spitting, are the reasons I couldn't stop laughing.

Still, it was otherwise not a good night, and in the morning there would be sad and hard decisions to be made. Because she was already on behavioral warning with the school, this new development didn't seem as funny to the administration as it was to us at that moment. She'd have to leave, which she did by her own choice, before there was a chance for it to be anyone else's.

———

The next fall, Rylee started at a new school and we started talking on the phone every day. It's hard to start a new college as a junior. Most people have their social situations pretty much figured out by that point. So she was lonely, and because I missed her a lot, I was, too. We were two hours apart now, but when we sat talking on the quads of our respective campuses we kind of figured out that we must be best friends because we just didn't like any of the people around us as much as we liked each other, which was a lot.

I visited her that fall on a three-day weekend. She was living at her parents' house and we sat on her childhood bed, looking through her diary from the previous year. She let me hold it and read it myself, which was one of those moments when you feel like somebody must really love you and you just want to squeeze them (nicely) until they burst. As I should have expected, having lived through our sophomore year myself, it was not a pleasant read. In one part she wrote about feeling like she wasn't really sure that she could trust me, or that we could ever be good friends. I knew, of course, that my own diary said things about her that were just as negative. But that didn't mean it didn't hurt to know she'd written angrily about me, too.

"Don't feel bad," she said when she saw my face. "I don't feel that way now."

We flipped through more pages until we got to the end, where I saw that she'd very neatly and carefully written out a list of what looked like the names of every boy she'd ever kissed, slept with, and/or dated. Rylee had made the list that summer, back when she was feeling pretty bad about its size, and at a time when I (regrettably, embarrassingly) might have judged her for it, too. Now I found it a treasure trove. The Dead Sea Scrolls, but more informative. Rylee's not a *Sex and the City* character, but considering that most of the list was just make-outs, it definitely wasn't small. "Oh my *God*," I said. "This is amazing." She even had a rating system—a "1" next to his name meant kissing plus, a "3" meant they had slept together, and a "2" meant some of that awkward stuff in between.

Going through those ratings made a lot of the things that seemed hard about the past year seem pretty funny, now that we were looking at it in list form. "You have accomplished a lot," I said. "My list would be pretty pathetic."

"You should make it," she said. She handed me a pen.

I have a little section in Rylee's diary now. My own little list of mishaps is written in the upper right-hand corner next to hers. It is a relatively small list, and sometimes, mostly for symmetrical purposes, I wish it were more expansive. To balance our achievement gap a little, I added a few non-boy-related collegiate escapades to my list: Cigarettes (3–7). The time I went out at 11:00 pm and was back throwing up on the floor, off of my top bunk, by 11:45. A particularly inappropriate Halloween costume. Or two.

This is not a list recorded for bragging rights, neither to grant them nor take them away. It is not a list of shames or regrets. It is just a list of some things we've done, bad and good and hot and weird, on our way to growing up.

I Think This Is Really about Coffee

EVERYBODY WHO WORKS IN A coffee shop is at least a little bit hot. Removed from that context of delicious smells and comfy chairs and blackboards with adorable drawings and handwriting on them, the employees might be just average looking. But there is something about baristas that is inescapably appealing. Maybe it's the aprons? I feel a little weird about saying I'm into boys wearing aprons, but I can't deny it. The transitive property of coffee-shop sex appeal works like this: A cute guy working in a coffee shop becomes a really hot guy, and an already-hot guy working in a coffee shop is hard to look at without hallucinating. He's glowing in rainbows! He's multiplying! He is the barista *and* all the customers. He's floating overhead. He's doing somersaults *while* floating overhead. No, he's just standing still. But he's standing in a way that no person has ever stood before. And I don't mean because of the apron.

When I was twenty, in the summer between my sophomore and junior years in college, I fell head over heels for a barista at my local coffee shop. His name was Sam, and he is the most beautiful boy I have ever seen—in *any* context—and I can promise you that if you saw him, he'd be the most beautiful boy you've ever seen, too. His good looks were beyond the court of public opinion. He looked like the result of a magical gay union between Patrick Dempsey and Freddie Prinze Jr. Think about that for a few minutes. Close the book and set it aside, then close your eyes, and just *think* about that. I will wait here. I'm actually going to take a few minutes to think about him, too.

All right. Calm down.

The first time I saw Sam, I was not prepared. I was wearing gym shorts, a T-shirt, and a sloppy ponytail. He commented on my shirt—it was, I'm sorry to say, one of those Urban Outfitters shirts that is like, "Yeah I AM a liberal so deal with it, THE MAN!"—and the first thing I thought was "Oh my God, he basically just looked at my boobs." (That was pretty much the first year I had boobs.) I somehow remembered enough words to order my coffee, and then I went to sit down in a booth while my friend Jenna ordered her drink. When Jenna came to sit down, we had a silent conversation about what had just happened, because our booth was fairly close to the counter where Sam stood working, perfectly and attractively.

"Whoa, super hot, right??" said Jenna's eyes.

"YES OMG OMG OMG AMAZING WHO IS THAT MAN??" said mine.

"You should talk to him again!!!" Jenna's eyebrows said.

"Whyyy did I dress like this today? Seriously. UGH," I said, by shaking my head and pressing my forehead with my fingers.

For the rest of our coffee date, Jenna and I talked (out loud) about whatever things we normally talked about then, but with a lot more laughter than would ever be necessary. We didn't explicitly plan it or anything, but I guess we were putting on a show. I was trying to send a subtle message to Sam (or, as we called him at that point, Barista Boy) by being as loud as humanly possible. "I am a girl, over here! I am funny and incredibly charming! Look how much fun I am having! My laughter is infectious, ha ha ha HA HAAAA!" I was trying to seduce him just by being physically *near* him. Like, seduction by osmosis. It works in movies constantly.

When we left, Sam said, "Thanks for coming in!" and I said, "Sure! Yeah! Thanks!" Jenna and I collected ourselves in the car and decided that we were going to have to come back as soon as possible. We had a summer project, all of a sudden. "This is going to be *just* like *Grease*," I said. "But with less stuff about cars."

The next time Jenna and I went into the coffee shop, it was in the evening. I wore my hair down and was dressed up like I had something to do besides lurk in a coffee shop trying to make the hottest boy of all time fall in love with me just by repeatedly appearing in front of his face. The shop was empty when we walked in, because 7:00 pm is not when most people enjoy having a coffee. This, of course, was part of the plan. I wanted to introduce myself, or us, rather, but I didn't want lots of people to be around wondering why this girl thought the employee serving her coffee really cared what her and her friend's names were. What hypothetical people might think in hypothetical situations has often bothered me a great deal.

Jenna and I walked up to the counter to a friendly and smiling Sam. We ordered our coffees and when we finished paying, I braced myself for my first big step, which turned out to be kind of like the steps Wile E. Coyote takes right off the edge of a cliff.

"By the way," I said, "I'm Jenna and this is Katie."

Time stopped. I ran around in circles. I screamed for twenty minutes and clutched at my eyeballs. I threw up three times. I prayed. I set a table on fire. When time started again, it seemed I had actually just spent a couple of seconds nervously laughing.

"I mean…haha…*I'm* Katie and *this* is Jenna. Ahhhh. Haha. Uhh. Yeah," I said, willing myself to spontaneously combust, pleading for the appearance of a black hole that would take us all back to five minutes earlier before we had even walked into the shop. It would just be better for everyone involved, I thought.

"Haha…I'm Sam. Nice to meet you," he said, but I didn't hear it, because his eyelashes were talking to me at the same time. "Look at us, just LOOK at us. We're real. Can you believe it? *Real.* Watch us open. Watch us close."

Jenna and I sat at a table right by the counter and started talking, but it was only moments before Sam and Ted, another barista there who Jenna decided was kind of cute as well— everything was falling into place now—asked if we wanted to challenge them in a word-scramble competition. Because I can't say no to competitions (at least ones I could feasibly win), and I definitely can't turn down opportunities to trash-talk hot guys (again, my idea of flirting is "being kind of mean"), I agreed. It ended up a tie, but from then on the four of us were kind of summer friends.

Jenna didn't work that summer and I was getting a maximum of fifteen to twenty hours a week at Victoria's Secret, glaring at customers who dared to pick up any of the underwear I spent literally *hours* folding, so the two of us had a lot of time to spend in coffee shops. That one coffee shop in particular. We probably went in two or three times a week. Sometimes we would get to talk to Sam and Ted for a couple of hours, if it was slow enough and their boss wasn't around. I learned that Sam, who was perfectly aged at twenty-three years old, had just graduated from a local Christian college, which made me a little nervous because that particular school is super conservative and I am not. I wrote about this concern in my journal, where I ended up very rationally concluding that "nobody that perfect-looking could be THAT conservative."

After a few weeks spent hanging out and talking (never alone, always with Jenna) and consulting every last one of my friends on what I should do (the consensus: do something, do ANYTHING), I decided to send Sam a friend request on Facebook. He accepted, and for the first few minutes, everything was great. Then I saw his relationship status, in slow motion. First I saw that he had one. Then, even worse, I saw that there was a name—a girl's name—linked at the end of it. I was both shocked and not very shocked at all. It seemed unfair (if not unlikely) that Sam could have spent hours talking to me, asking me questions, giving me (and only me) free drinks, and smiling with dimples at me without having some kind of interest in me. But also, we had only hung out in a context where he was being paid. Yes, talking to Jenna and me was probably, in some way or another, better than mopping the floor no matter what he thought of us. And sure, this sort of shit seemed to happen to me constantly. I had no reason to expect that this venture of mine could have gone any better. I had just wanted it to. I had just thought that maybe the wanting it badly could have been enough.

I clicked on his apparent girlfriend's name for a quick and perfunctory background check. What did she look like? (Pretty.) How long had they been dating? (Literally forever; since birth, seemingly.) Did it seem like maybe something dramatic was about to happen, like he'd realize he hated her because what he *really* wanted was a twenty-year-old tall brunette whom he'd known for a month, one who talked about Harry Potter too much and seemed only passingly familiar with her own name? Did it seem like he'd then break up with his girlfriend and, when the aforementioned girl came into the coffee shop he'd give her her regular chai for free with, like, a diamond ring at the bottom of it? And that then she'd drink the whole thing only to be like, "What...is this chunk that won't come through the straw, gross," and then realize that she was ENGAGED NOW?? (Hard to say from a handful of pictures of his girlfriend, but not really, no.)

I felt a little betrayed. I felt that if Sam had wanted me to know he had a girlfriend, she would have come up in conversation by that midway point in the summer. I guess that's not always true—people in couples don't always go around announcing "my boyfriend" this and "my girlfriend" that, and if they did, I'd probably be throwing up so much all the time that it wouldn't even be worth it to go outside ever. Lots of people actually do that, excessively, and I hate them every time. So it is a damned-if-you-do/cry-about-it-if-you-don't-type situation.

Jenna and I kept going into the coffee shop like nothing had changed, and nothing really did. The girlfriend never came up in conversation, still, even at times when it would have been perfectly appropriate and normal for him to talk about her—like when going over what he had done the past weekend. Of course, I interpreted his continued silence on the topic as a signal to keep hoping that he was going to break up with her or that, at the least, he had an illicit crush on me, too. He certainly acted like it, at times. A randomized poll found that one hundred percent of my friends to whom I described his actions and our conversations agreed with me on that one.

At some point after our "friendship" (ugh) became Facebook official, Sam started writing me messages. He would mostly just refer to things we'd talked about the last time we hung out at the coffee shop, sending me YouTube links or asking me how my halfhearted attempts at summer tennis practice were going. My messages back to him were almost always longer, because I figured that asking him a million questions should, in theory, increase the likelihood that he'd respond. I don't know why I worried about that, though, because he always did. Sam always asked me questions back, too. He would say things like, "Hey where were you the other night? Ted and I missed you guys in the store." He was a real asshole like that.

At the end of the summer, Jenna and I went into the shop one last time to say our good-byes. We had talked around the idea of doing something—playing tennis, getting food—outside the coffee shop with Sam and Ted, but it just never happened. She and I went in toward closing time, about a week before we had to head back to our respective colleges. Ted wasn't in and Sam was sweeping the nearly empty shop when we got there. He made us our last drinks (well, not our *last*, but the last ones we'd ever get that were touched by his fingers), and we tried to think about appropriate ways to end our little barista/customer/friend/crush relationship. I landed on "It was nice meeting you and hanging out this summer." He nodded. "Yeah, definitely." He'd almost always been behind the counter, whenever we talked, until that night. Outside it, the smallest bit of coffee-shop magic faded. He was a little shorter than I'd always thought.

Sure enough, once I went back to school—once he was no

longer my barista—the Facebook messages started to taper off, and eventually I sent one that went unanswered. After two weeks went by (a grace period), I sent out the alert to my friends: a text reading "aobtd." This is our code for when everything with a boy all of a sudden turns to shit and it's time for everyone to chime in about how terrible he was anyway. It stands for "another one bites the dust." And though I couldn't have fairly expected anything else from a customer service–based acquaintance with a girlfriend, I was still sad. Not ugly-cry sad, but disappointed all the same. He was just so hot.

It's for the best, right? I think it's for the best. It would never have worked. He was too religious, too weirdly Libertarian. He had never read Harry Potter and, despite the relatively high frequency with which I pitched it, had zero interest in starting. And also maybe the part where he had a serious girlfriend. All of it, swept under the rug in an instant just for an incredibly hot boy with perfect eyelashes and perfect hair and a perfect face who gave me free coffee sometimes.

Actually, when I put it that way, I can't be blamed for trying. Nor can any of my friends who have also tried to date their baristas. But that doesn't mean it isn't a very, very bad idea.

———

Jenna likes coffee even more than I do. I get by on a cup every morning (with the occasional bonus on days when I'm angry with the world), but she makes entire pots of it for herself in the mornings, sometimes buying an extra latte to get through the afternoon and evening. Both of us believe that coffee is a necessary evil. Actually, I don't think either of us thinks of it as evil. It's more like a necessary and delicious treasure. It fixes crankiness, it fixes tiredness, it fixes headaches, it (sort of) fixes hangovers. What's that you say? Coffee creates as many problems as it "fixes"? You just SHUT THE HELL UP.

It took a couple summers, but eventually Jenna fell in love (not love—caffeine addiction?) with her own barista. His name was Brian. Jenna went into the Starbucks where he worked almost every afternoon late that summer, while she was working as a part-time intern and studying for the GRE. Brian was boyish looking, with curly golden-brown hair. He was quiet and had a nervous smile. He was one of those boys who are basically made to have crushes on—boys for whom there is no obvious descriptor other than "adorable." At least at first.

Brian got in the habit of giving Jenna free lattes (they always get you with the free drinks) and sitting with her for a few minutes when business was slow. Jenna doesn't remember what they talked about those first few times, but she knows it seemed there was a lot to say. When you talk to someone beautiful for three to five minutes at a time, it is *incredible* how much you can have in common.

One day when Brian's shift was ending and Jenna was in the shop, he asked her if she wanted to come with him to a sports bar, to meet up with his friends and watch the Twins game. Jenna very bravely said sure, and packed her things up on the spot. She texted me on the sly throughout the evening.

Katie:"How is it going??????????????"

Jenna:"Good! He is so cute! We have so much to talk about!"

Katie:"OMG OMG OMG! Yay! Tell me everythingggggg."

Jenna:"We mostly are just talking about the Twins! Aaaand
he's telling me something about beer hops. He seems really
into hops. But OMG so cuuuuuuute."
Katie:"Huh…okay. But amazing! Hooray!"

Jenna and Brian didn't kiss that first night, but they
exchanged phone numbers and made plans to hang out again.
She and I met for dinner (or more coffee, probably) and recapped
those first few dates. We're only able to figure things out over
food. The girl was infatuated. She was like, "I really see things
working out with him, we have so much in common, even when
we're not talking it's so comfortable just being with him, he is
so CUTE, and free coffee," et cetera, et cetera. They had about
two weeks of honeymooning as a new couple. But from then on,
it was one disaster after another.

The relationship's three-week check-in point, relayed to
me over burritos: "He smokes weed pretty much every day,"
Jenna told me. "He likes to smoke weed and talk to me about
Buddhism, kind of a lot."

Our one-month evaluation was spent eating ice cream in a
McDonald's parking lot, which is the main thing we have to
eat—and it is not a choice, not really—when things are VERY
SERIOUS: "He says he's not really into labels and that's why he
doesn't want to call me his girlfriend. But I don't know, should that
matter if we've agreed to be exclusive? I asked him at what point he
usually felt comfortable using 'girlfriend' and he said maybe not
until several months have gone by," she said. I nodded in empathy.

Five weeks: "He told me he's really confident in his sex skills.
I wasn't blown away."

Six weeks: "He weirdly told me about his sex confidence again. I'm like, 'Is this a repeat-it-until-it's-true-type scenario?'"

At two months, it seemed like Jenna was reaching the breaking point, when literally everything a person does is annoying because it's not so much about the little things themselves as the fact that the little things remind you of the fact that you're dating someone horrible. He wore a baseball hat always, and it was *always* cocked to the side. He called his mom "Mum," inexplicably. He got embarrassingly drunk on red wine in a classy pub, and Jenna had to help him walk to her car. Worst of all, by far, he was overly fond of the term "splooge." (A hint: Using that word even once makes you overly fond of it.) For example, when they were having sex, he would say to Jenna, "Ahhhh, I'm going to splooge!" I am not sure how she didn't just close down her vagina for business right then and there. Mine had to take, like, three sick months just hearing about it from her. I feel off even now.

Then there was the night when Jenna got a little tipsy and spilled all of her emotions into Brian's bed while they lay there together, post make-out but pre–anything else. "I told him about my family issues, the time I was really really sick, my worries about my future, my job stress, all of it," she told me, over coffee, the source of it all, the next day.

"How did he respond?" I asked.

"He asked me for a hand job."

The end was nigh. Jenna, however, doesn't enjoy the breakup. She mostly dealt with Brian in passive-aggression, inventing reasons why they couldn't hang out tonight, or tomorrow night, or really any night this week. Or next, for that matter. I begged her to just break up with him for real already. I told her to just tell him how she felt, to just be direct.

"Yeah, but I mean, how do you tell someone they're really boring and stupid?" she asked.

Eventually he broke up with her instead. And then, months later, he tried to get back together with her, the way the worst ones always do. But the steam had cleared, and she had moved on. On the other side, she was a different person. Now she substitutes green or chamomile tea for a few of those cups of coffee. It just got to be too much.

Boys with Girlfriends

THERE IS SOMETHING ELSE I should have taken away from the summer I spent infatuated with an essentially betrothed barista, and that is that it is a waste of time to have a crush on someone who already has someone else. And if that seems like it should be obvious, then you aren't consulting your own version of the handful of brazenly optimistic friends/coworkers/hairstylists I'm prone to consulting in cases like these. They say the same things every time: that "people break up," and "a girlfriend isn't a wife," and a handful of similar short observations based on anecdotal evidence that, while technically true at the most basic level, are dubious at best—for several reasons, not the least of which is the perplexing notion that my total inability to woo anyone single would coexist with wanton, seductive boyfriend-stealing capabilities—but which are just vaguely promising enough to make you (or, fine, me) think that liking the person you were already determined to like could be worth it.

So at the very end of my senior year in college, when I had a crush on someone with a girlfriend and mostly everyone told me it was totally legitimate, I ran with it. (Well, I hesitantly tiptoed with it.) Because maybe it was true, because college was basically over and I didn't know what was next, and also, perhaps mostly, because he was extremely dreamy. In, like, a non-obvious sort of way, obscured by clothes and hair and near-silence and general unavailability. You'll see. You'll get it, maybe.

———————

It didn't help that I'd been harboring illusions about Jim, off and on, for two years.

I'd seen him first during my sophomore year, in the writing center where I worked as a tutor. His appointment that day was with someone else, which was bad in that I didn't get to talk directly to him, but good in that it left me free to sit at an adjacent table and glance repeatedly at him for the better part of forty-five minutes. After he left, multiple attempts at sensual eye contact gone unnoticed, I checked the center's appointment book to try to find his name, but had no luck. (A mystery man— I love those.) As it goes with so many of my stranger-crushes, he was designated with a nickname so that I could refer to him by code. I had thought he kind of looked like Jim Halpert from *The Office*. So that is pretty much the whole story of how I came up with "Jim Halpert Boy."

Jim Halpert Boy is one of the most elusive crushes I have ever had. He was his own endangered species. After that first sighting in the writing center, I'd go months at a time without seeing him around campus. At a school of two thousand students with a campus you could see one end of from the other, this just didn't happen all that often. The infrequent sightings only made the crush intensify. It was like a *Where's Waldo* scenario in which

I felt personally vindicated each time I spotted him. One sighting outside the library could keep me going for another month, easy.

My tennis teammate Sarah had this knack for saying all the wrong things at the wrong times, but still I shared my secrets—in this case, Jim—with her because a) I tell everyone everything regardless, and b) she was a year older, and incredibly enthusiastic about her younger teammates' so-called love lives. She herself couldn't keep a secret, but still I couldn't stop. I had told her about my escapades with Dylan "Homework" Campbell, and she promptly brought it up to our whole team at the next practice, while the boys' team also practiced mere yards away. "SARAH!!!!!!!!!!!!!" I whisper-yelled. "Could you *please* shut UP?!?!?" "What??" she said. "They aren't paying attention to us." I glared at her. Apparently *she* didn't know about that abomination of the senses in which cute boys can hear you speak their names from literally any distance in space and/or time.

Still, I told Sarah about Jim Halpert Boy right away. He was really more of a vapor than a person anyway, so it felt safe, I guess. She also had no idea who he was. But a few weeks later, when Sarah and I went to the campus sandwich shop after tennis practice to get dinner, I saw him sitting at a table nearby.

"*Sarah,*" I hissed out of the side of my mouth.

"What?" she said.

"SHHHHHH. *Jim Halpert Boy, six o'clock.*"

"What's at six? I can't hear you."

"Just…just…shut up!!! *Jim…Halpert…Boy. Behind us.*" I jerked my head backward, and then started playing with my hair to give the appearance of being nonchalant. I practically tore the hair out of my own head.

"OH MY GOD WHERE?!" she basically screamed.

"I hate you," I said. "I hope something terrible happens to you."

She looked around for a minute while I stared straight ahead, willing him not to notice her searching. I peered at her out of the corner of my eye and saw that she had fixed on the approximate spot where "Jim" sat behind me, eating a sandwich, gorgeously.

"The one in the...camo?" she asked, in a voice that I would actually describe as a little bit bitchy.

It was true: Jim wore a lot of camo. Sometimes on the top AND the bottom (!). He also wore a lot of paisley, and a lot of bandannas, and a lot of dark-brown-with-black. After so many years spent witnessing straight boys in their natural habitat, a girl must accept that, frequently, such errors in judgment come with the territory. Sure, usually there weren't *quite* so many errors assembled like a smorgasbord of patterns and prints onto one person's body. But I could overlook these things, especially when it was clear that the arms underneath them would have NO trouble carrying me out of a burning building, should the need ever arise.

But there was also the problem of his hair. More often than not, actually, I've been attracted to boys in spite of their hair. Jim was no exception.

He seemed to be in the routine of growing out his hair to the point of being unable to see through it, then *perming it*, then shaving it all off to start the entire cycle of terror over again. Look, I don't begrudge a man who does shit to his hair. A little bit of product can be nice. I appreciate boys who don't have bangs they allow to sit flat on their foreheads like sad little Spock hair. If someone were to draw a line when it comes to men's hairstyles, I would agree that "No perms, if at all possible" is a pretty fair one. I followed Jim on over to the other side anyway, like a sick puppy with terrible taste in guys. But still, we never met.

Then two years went by, and it was May of my senior year. One day, Jim and a friend simply strolled up to the tennis court where I was playing a match with my friend Jane and asked if we wanted to play doubles.

I hadn't really given Jim much of a second thought since sophomore year. He was always *there*, always a hot person stored in my mind, but I had long since given up the idea that anything would ever happen. I'd stopped looking semi-wildly for him whenever I went somewhere on campus I'd seen him before. I'd been through approximately six other crushes since then, but none of that mattered now. The disappearing act formerly known as my most mysterious sophomore-year crush had come up to *me*, seemingly voluntarily, and asked if my friend and I would like to play tennis with them. And, implicitly, like, look at each other.

After that first match, the four of us started playing tennis a few times a week. In between our matches, Jim and I texted each other, having gotten each other's numbers for match-scheduling purposes. I've spent a lot of time trying to remember what we talked about so much, because Jim did not actually have a lot to say. My brain told me this was because he was "astonishingly dim," as one of my friends put it. My heart told me it was because he was the "strong and silent" type. (A type I'm starting to think isn't even a real thing??) I know we trash-talked about baseball. This is another one of those things that I always think of as clearly flirtatious, and I'm not really sure why. "Your team sucks," I'd say. "No, *your* team sucks," he'd say. And so on.

What I do remember, quite clearly, is being smacked in the shin by a tennis ball that Jim served in one of our doubles matches. I wasn't even in the service box. I wasn't even on the receiving side of the court, but this is how boys play sports when they don't completely know how; hit everything as hard as you can. It doesn't matter where.

When the ball hit me I screamed, "JIMMMMM!!!" (except I used his real name) and jumped around laughing. He, holding back laughter, asked if I was okay. This is one of the many reasons why tennis is the most flirtatious sport in the world. The likelihood that you will mildly injure your partners and then have to coddle them afterward is high. Ideally there would be no begging involved. Ideally.

After our match that night I sent him a text.

"My leg hurts. I think you need to make it up to me."

"Oh yeah? What did you have in mind?"

"I think I should get a free shot at you." (I was going for the threatening-injury-is-sexy approach here, apparently. I am embarrassed for me, too.)

"Or I could just buy you a shot." (Oh, that's more normal.)

"That works too. :)"

A lot of students from my school went to this local hole-in-the-wall karaoke bar on Monday nights for two-dollar beers. I didn't usually see Jim there, but when my friends and I showed up that night, I recognized some of his friends standing around the dart boards and got my hopes up. I texted him to ask if he was coming out that night, to which he responded, "I'm going to try." I could practically feel his muffled enthusiasm vibrating, halfheartedly, through my phone.

He did show up, in the company of a girl who, until then, I had only partially feared was his girlfriend, having seen her in a couple of his Facebook pictures and heard bits of gossip from a mutual friend who had a class with him the previous semester. That night it seemed pretty clear that she *was* his girlfriend as I peered, out of my peripherals, at her, petite and pretty and blond, leaning against him and touching those goddamn arms. And that is when I should have given up and gone home early to have a snack and watch the New Year's Eve episode of *The O.C.* or something. I should have started burrowing right then. But what I did instead was to walk over to him at some point when the possible girlfriend was otherwise occupied and say hi. He turned to me and said: "Let's get you that shot."

Either I am the expert on crushing on non-single boys with questionable loyalty to their girlfriends, or I am the expert on mistakenly interpreting friendliness for flirtation. I suspect it's a little bit of both, but the important point is that I am an EXPERT. And I should have known, I can't say that enough. I really should have known. But here was someone I'd had a crush on (however on and off) for two years offering to buy me a drink. The tunnel vision that kind of long-awaited victory can give you is incredible. We only stood there a few minutes, just long enough for him to buy me a shot, for us to drink them, and for a few moments of awkward (but thrilling) grinning afterward, but I couldn't see anybody else. Least of all a girlfriend. That just wouldn't make sense.

He and I played a singles match a few days later—my idea, the kind of boldness I can only come up with when pressed by the circumstances, like when I am in my last ten days of college and therefore in my (potential) last few chances at true romance with Jim Halpert Boy, the myth, the man, the legend—and when we were done, as we were picking up the tennis balls, Jim paused by the fence and said, "You got me in trouble the other night."

"With the lady?" I said, without thinking. I knew. I knew who he meant even as I was still pretending she wasn't who she very clearly was.

"Yeah," he said. "I think she was a bit jealous."

"As well she should have been, for you are a dog and a scoundrel and I will be excusing myself at this very moment! Good DAY!" is what I should have said.

"Oh yeah? Just because you bought a girl a shot?" is what I actually said. And that is the very worst part. That is the part I want to erase most of all. Because I was trying to sound cooler and more laid-back than his girlfriend, and first of all there was no conceivable way I could have been, and second of all I didn't know her. It wasn't a conscious decision to say it, and I was speaking before I knew what else would come out of my mouth, but that had to be it. Because that is a fucking stupid thing to say. There is no "just because" about it, not in this case. She would have had all sorts of reasons to be suspicious. And knowing that, hearing him tell me that, was electrifying. It's the worst I've ever felt about feeling good.

We walked over to the net, one of us on either side.

"I kind of wish I wasn't going abroad next week," he said. "It's been fun playing tennis with you guys, and you seem like a cool girl."

"Thanks," I said. He wasn't really saying that much, there. Just enough.

I told Jim to send me a postcard from abroad, and a week and a day later, I sent him a Facebook message and asked him how he was liking the trip. He said it was good, but that the girls there weren't as cute as he expected, probably because of the lack of tennis skirts. At the end of that sentence there was a wink-face emoticon. Obviously.

Weeks passed, and he returned to the U.S., but the postcard never came. So, because I like to embarrass myself as thoroughly as possible, I asked him, only half joking, to send me one from his hometown to make it up to me. (I'd like to explain my reasoning to you, here. I really would. But that would require first that I remember it, and second that I could recognize it as based in a normal human understanding of logic and pride.) Two weeks later I got a picture of him and his dog in the mail, with the edges whited out like it was snowing. "What is this?" I said to myself, again and again, wandering around, for days. "What *is* this?"

I threw it away. ~~At least I can claim that much.~~ (...Juuust kidding? I actually found it buried in a desk drawer, just now, because I thought I should check to be sure I remembered that right. Ugh. It was even worse than I remembered. But THEN I threw it away. I took a picture of it, texted it to three of my friends, and then I threw it away.)

In the middle of July, Jenna and I drove out to visit friends in the Chicago suburbs, and while we were out I decided to text Jim to see if he wanted to stop by the bar. I had heard that he and his girlfriend had broken up. (I didn't know it at the time, but it was she who broke up with him, of course.) They'd apparently done this already a few times that summer, but it seemed like this time it was going to stick. He told me he was about an hour out of the area, and I said that's okay, not a big deal. Then he texted me to say he was coming out anyway. It was ten. He'd be there by eleven-thirty.

And the craziest part of the whole damn story is that he was.

We sat next to each other in the booth, side-eyeing and laughing about nothing. He smelled good, like smoke and bubble gum, but in a good way. When we left, my crafty friend Bri told him he should stay over at her parents' house with Jenna and me. It was far too late to drive home. Bri and Jenna led the way to Bri's house, and I, for no real reason at all, rode with Jim. To "help navigate." I can barely find the grocery store in my own hometown, but that doesn't matter. Jim didn't know that. On the drive we talked about how he wanted to be a firefighter, and I knew that I had at least been right about the carrying-me-out-of-a-building part of this mess, if nothing else.

He slept on the couch in Bri's basement. I slept on an air mattress two feet away. Jenna slept on an air mattress three feet away from that. In secret, when he wasn't nearby, Jenna had asked me if I wanted her to sleep up in Bri's room with her. My eyes widened, I shook my head. "No," I said. *"Stay. Here."*

I don't know how to explain that. I really don't.

But let me try. I wanted something to happen, but I also didn't necessarily want anything to happen. I wanted to make out with him but not have sex with him. Or I wanted to have sex with him, but not right then. Not in my friend's parents' basement. I wanted him to know that I liked him, but I didn't want it to be TOO obvious. I didn't want to force it. I wanted his driving an hour to see me late at night to mean that he wanted to date me (even though he was still in college and now, all of a sudden, I wasn't, even though we barely knew each other, even though he had *just* broken up with his girlfriend), not that he just wanted to have sex. I wanted everything to be different than what all the evidence around me suggested was going on, which was that Jim was dumb, and I, for persisting this long, was even dumber.

In the morning the four of us went out for breakfast, and I hugged him good-bye when he left to drive home. He said, "Maybe I'll have to make the trip out to Minnesota sometime." He shouldn't have said that.

We exchanged a few more Facebook messages, mine never bringing up a visit directly but written with the idea that if he saw my name a few more times, he would remember what he'd said and how much he wanted to see me again. He responded every time, at first. But my practical side knew it was over, really. I started reading *One Hundred Years of Solitude*, for symbolism. My dreamy side kept hoping. I kept thinking, just give it one more day. One more day, and the perfect text message or Facebook message will arrive and it will be different. I was wrong all week.

The next message in my inbox was so bad that I didn't even want to respond. It wasn't mean or rude or cold. It just wasn't anything at all. So I stopped.

According to my journal, the next thing I did was go out and buy an extraordinarily tiny bright green bikini for twenty dollars from Victoria's Secret. I think that because I bought it on clearance I accepted a degree of smallness I wouldn't have otherwise, and I didn't wear it once that summer. But just knowing it was there—that helped a little.

————

I never consciously thought about this at the time, but have decided since that it is true: Liking someone who already has a girlfriend is just easier. These aren't choices made on the scene, not knowingly. Sam and Jim both had girlfriends, but I didn't know that when I first saw them. I liked them (or the way they looked, anyway) first, and THEN I learned that they weren't really free to be liked. And that didn't make me like them more, I don't think, but it didn't make me like them less. It made me aware that there were certain lines I shouldn't cross in my interactions with them, but those are usually the lines I'm afraid of crossing anyway. Those are the lines that say I shouldn't touch these people, or compliment the way they look, or hint vaguely at sexy stuff we could do if they weren't with someone else. That is fine with me. I honestly would not even know where to start.

So I'd wait, and do the littlest things, and then when nothing happened, I couldn't be too surprised or too heartbroken. I'm not allowed, because I knew nothing could happen. I didn't believe, but I knew. And I am so used to nothing happening. But at least when there's a previous girlfriend involved, and when me and him as an idea is even more over than it was when it started, I can point directly at the reason.

At the time, this always helps. It still hurts a lot—not a little—but it hurts less.

When you and I like someone who is already taken, a lot of our friends assume—based almost always on nothing—that we'd be better for him than the person he's already with, and what they really mean is that we should get what we want just because we want it. (Which is nice of all of us to say, but is also stupid. Not everybody gets everyone they want. In fact, I am pretty sure that almost nobody does. It's very annoying.) And if you hear it enough it starts to sound true, or at least true-ish. "Yes," we'll think. "This *does* seem like a worthwhile investment of time and emotion and ill-advised text messages." It starts to sound almost easier to hope for someone who already has a girl-friend than for someone who is single. A single person could choose literally anyone. Someone with a girlfriend has two choices: his girlfriend, or you. This, of course, is not even a little bit true. But it feels like it at the time.

It just isn't as scary to like someone who, if or when he doesn't like you back, you could say doesn't like you back because he *can't*.

I would like to tell you that two days later I was over it and mortified and working on recovery in a hole beneath the earth's crust. And mostly that is true. But two months later, in early October when I was back at school for Homecoming weekend, I texted Jim Halpert Boy to see if he was coming out to the bars. It wasn't about wanting to pretend there was a chance I'd still date him anymore. It was about drunkenness and making out and the mania associated with having realized I was no longer in college and would never again have this kind of easy access to boys. So I texted him against the advice of literally everyone, and when he replied "Nah,"—like an asshole, by the way, the worst, laziest fucking way to say no, aggravated texting crime #1—"hangin with the gf," I just laughed. Out loud, *and* in response. "Haha, ok," I texted back. "Have a good night." It was the exact way it should have ended, you know? I loved that text message, in a way where it was also the worst. It was exactly the thing I should have always known would be the last thing he'd ever say to me. It couldn't have been scripted better.

Part Four

♥   ♥   ♥

GRAD SCHOOL

Now I Hate Spruce Trees

I F I'M BEING TOTALLY HONEST (and I suppose I might as well continue to do so at this point), one little, tiny, minuscule part of the reason I decided to go back to graduate school was so that I could fall in love. It was second (fifty-seventh, really) to the desires to learn more, to become better qualified for what I thought I wanted to do with my life, to assuage my college nostalgia, and to make more friends, but that silliest reason was there all the same. Sorry, parents. Sorry, pursuit of knowledge. Sorry, Sallie Mae. It is the sad truth.

It took me exactly six months of living with my parents and working various short-term jobs in predominantly middle-aged female workplaces to decide that I had had enough of the "real world" and wished to return to living in some kind of bubble—where everyone would be young and hot and studying and making out—as soon as possible. It didn't matter that four years of college had not been enough to arrange a meet-cute with the man of my dreams—it would be autumn, when we were both strolling across campus with our arms full of books, only to collide into one another, softly and gently, eyes meeting over the mess we'd made, delirious with the heady smell of textbook paper—but surely two years of graduate school would do the trick. Boys (men?) there would be a little older, a lot smarter, and, most likely, one billion times hotter. They just *had* to be. They would probably also have one very important trait that none of the boys I liked in college seemed to have: an interest in dating me.

So because I missed being around young people and boys, and because I was interested in being a student again and having goals that I understood, and because I was, I promise, actually interested in the coursework and learning how to further my career, I decided to apply to graduate school. Plus, I've always really liked workbooks. My GRE book was no exception, despite its rather alarming attempts at geometry humor. I even convinced Rylee to join me for the whole thing. She was interested in a program similar to mine, and I was interested in having my best friend with me in my home state for two years (and more, if I could subtly make her fall in love with it by pointing out all the nice lakes and everything) and pretending that we were in college together all over again.

She and I moved in together and I walked over to school on the first day of orientation and right into an enormous mess. He was in my group that first day, skinny and tall. Unlike almost every other crush I've had, I learned his name on the very same day that I torpedoed into one of my progressive bouts of infatuation. I never used it, though—well, not to anyone but him. Instead, obviously, I used a code name. My new grad-school friend Marie would pick it out while we studied statistics in the lounge. "Spruce," she said. "Because he's tall. Like a spruce tree."

Though we technically met on our first day at school, Spruce and I didn't talk to each other until a full month later. It was one of those weird things where two people know they know each other's names and realize, inwardly, that they should probably be acknowledging each other's presence, but decide not to anyway. It's never clear who's responsible for these decisions. It's all one person being too scared to say hi to the other, and then the other being all, "Well I can't say hi NOW or she/he will think I am an actual serial killer," and then the first person feels justified by her/his decision but also a little sad because, hello, does the other person not remember that they've MET before? And then both people just keep ignoring one another for the most part, but also making fairly intense and regular eye contact, from safe distances, until the effort to not say hello like normal human beings becomes too conspicuous and introductions must be made. It was like that for us. We looked at each other, across the classroom, every Monday and Wednesday morning, and sometimes in the hall. I kept trying to explain, via eye language, that he should come talk to me already. His eyes were like, "No, YOU." It was a disaster.

We met (for real) because Rylee made me sit down with him at a happy hour after school. First we sort of pranced around the perimeters, her telling me to just pick somewhere to sit like a normal person and me putting too much thought into which table would seem like I hadn't thought too much about it. Toward ten o'clock, Rylee told me that if we didn't go over to his table, where a small group had formed, we were leaving. And I do usually respond well to ultimatums. So we pulled up chairs to the group (where two other students we knew sat, thankfully) and introductions went all around, and he said, "Me and Katie are practically old friends. We had orientation together, do you remember?" And I was a goner from there on out. He said my name in a way that put us in a pair. I couldn't hear much of anything else for a while, because I wasn't listening to anybody, but I know that at some point it came up that Rylee and I played tennis and were thinking about starting an informal tennis club—an idea that Spruce enthusiastically supported. (They always get you with the tennis!) He told us to keep him posted. When he left he said, "Katie, always a pleasure," which was simultaneously bizarre and adorable. He fit that description a lot.

The next day in statistics lab he sat near us, and asked us if we still wanted to play tennis. We exchanged phone numbers and agreed to play the next day, Saturday afternoon. It would be a doubles match: Rylee and I against Spruce and a friend of his. Then, someone (I can't remember who) suggested we switch up the teams: Rylee and the friend, Spruce and me. It was perfect. We talked just enough for me to know that I was basically in love, but not enough for me to know any real information about him, except for the fact that he had incredible cheekbones—which is really all I needed to know anyway, right? A good set of cheekbones can take care of me, encourage me, make me laugh, raise my children.

He asked us to go out with him that night, to a bar in Minneapolis where he was meeting some other friends. Conveniently, we had no other plans. I was over the moon, and Rylee was over the moon for me. And if you are having trouble understanding why this was monumental (because it was, it just was), remember that this was the first time ever that I'd had a crush that seemed like it might actually turn into something more plausible than it once was. For starters, we met, which, I was coming to learn, was a really important first step. We were talking to each other, and easily. He was single. But not only that; we exchanged numbers, we hung out, and then he asked me (okay, fine, us) to hang out again. In the same DAY.

The bar was too perfect to be true. There was a drinking spelling bee going on, and Spruce was participating, so we sat at a booth with his friends (all girls, all coupled, thank GOD) and watched him spell. Every time he came back to the booth I'd get to make more of that eye contact with him, only now it was better because I knew him and I could smile as big and happy as I felt. He smiled big at me, too. Because he kept getting up to participate in the bee, our conversation was in nervous, hard-to-hear segments on disconnected topics, as if we were playing *Jeopardy!* He was Alex Trebek. Animals, for 100 points: Are wolves better, or bears? Politics, for 500: Your favorite constitutional amendment is? The Nineteenth, I picked—the one that granted women's suffrage. He nodded and smiled. "Mine, too." That's a gold medal for a political science feminist nerd like me. The easiest, weirdest pickup line. I know I'm gushing, but it was just so goddamn great. I mean, we played cat's cradle. His friend had string with her (?? Artists.), and after she and I played a couple rounds, Spruce told us that he didn't know how to play. So of course I taught him, hand grazing more than what was necessary to the game's function, giggling like an infatuated maniac. Don't even try to tell me that if that scene took place in a movie starring Zooey Deschanel and Joseph Gordon-Levitt, it wouldn't make 300 billion dollars. You cannot get any more sickeningly twee-cute. If I had been watching any other boy and girl play cat's cradle in a bar booth, I would have been like, "Are you fucking kidding me?" But it was me and him, so I just beamed all night, and probably for several days after. When Rylee and I left that night, he shook our hands. See? Bizarre. Adorable.

The week after that, we played tennis again. But when we didn't do anything else over the weekend because he didn't ask us to (and I...well I didn't suggest anything for the same reasons I ate that smoky chip, which is to say I have a problem), I panicked. If it seemed to be too good to be true, I figured it was. I called the support team, which is what my group of friends turn into when I have a crush for which I need consistent analysis and encouragement. Each friend serves a special purpose: I have Rylee to address things from a heartfelt and cautiously optimistic but reasonable angle. When asked if a Spruceless weekend meant that "everything is ruined," she is apt to say something like, "No, it doesn't. It's one week, it's fine. Just remember that he's a student, too, maybe he has work to do, and he is from here so he has other friends. He is still enthusiastic about seeing you at tennis and school. Just be patient." I have Bri to be unreservedly enthusiastic, to reply to any/all concerns with "Oh my God, don't even, he is so clearly already in love with you and just waiting for the go-ahead to declare it. People don't just, like, make all that eye contact for nothing." I have Colleen to talk circles around herself and to stress me out further, if I'm feeling like I want to be really stressed out (which happens more than you might think). I have Jenna to echo my concerns back to me and make me feel justified in being crazy: "I would be worried, too. But you shouldn't worry, but I would be worried, too. Totally reasonable." And then I have two or three people on reserve who are probably less invested but whose advice I'll seek anyway when I'm truly desperate for positive feedback. They're benchwarmers who would probably leave the field, if only I'd let them.

My love/depression-themed iTunes playlist got SUCH a workout that week.

On a chart of this "relationship's" progression, we would have been just barely above the x-axis at this point. (But also, somehow, the line was so much higher up than what it must have looked like with me and everyone else I ever liked.) We had met, and he didn't visibly detest me, so we weren't negative. We'd had a bit of a downturn after the previous weekend's excitement, but I still felt good, some of the time. It was a hospital-monitor heart rate. But the next weekend took the chart to new heights. It was exciting but also terribly nerve-wracking. You know, like the top of a rollercoaster. Right before you plummet to your death.

Rylee was going to be out of town that weekend, so I dragged Jenna to that week's Thursday night happy hour with me. There we talked to Spruce and another couple of people from my school, and I launched into this extended...bit, I guess, about the taxidermied animal heads posted around the bar, and for once felt that I came off more charming than strange. He was laughing, anyway, and touching my arm for emphasis that wasn't really needed. He told me that I was intimidating, I can't remember why. This stunned me. Did he remember how many times I'd already talked about *Star Wars* and *The X-Files* in his presence? I thought that *and* asked him that, that's how stunned I was. Still, I took it as a good sign, if a bewildering one: I made *him* nervous or uneasy? I wasn't aware that was possible. So at the end of the night, because I had prepared for this and told myself to make use of this Rylee-less weekend, I told him he should call me the next day. I said, "Let me know if you're doing anything this weekend because Rylee's out of town and I will be bored." He looked a little taken aback, but he said sure, of course, definitely.

I was so proud of myself.

On Friday he texted me to tell me a guy we knew from school was having a party and that he'd call when he was on the way over. I was calmer than I always thought I'd be, probably because I still didn't know what was going on. Was it a date, or wasn't it? When he called, he told me the party was near my apartment, and did I want him to stop by my apartment to pick me up on the way? (Yes, please, obviously.) He had biked over, and I still remember him sitting on a fence when I came downstairs, jumping off when he saw me. On the walk over he told me he was glad he wore a big coat because then he could seem bigger if we saw any troublemaking teens on the walk there. It seemed like a date.

When we got to the party, we hung up our coats and I said hi to a few people I knew from school. I went to buy a cup for the keg, but Spruce handed me one before I could. "I already bought yours, sorry! I shouldn't have presumed..." he trailed off. I smiled and told him thanks. One point for "Yes, this is a date." For the no side: five points. Just because I don't trust anybody or myself.

Though we separated sometimes to walk around the party and talk to other people, we always came back to each other. He put his arm around me when trying to decide how much taller than me he was (about three inches: perfect). I touched his arm. It was very scandalous. I was a little bit drunk on crappy keg beer, so when an undergrad in a hockey uniform started chatting me up, I was snappier toward him than I might normally have been. He was wasted, and he got a little too close to me, and before I knew it, Spruce was on the scene, lightly telling him, in so many words, to back off. I feel like such a failure for liking that a boy came to my defense, especially since I normally love to handle my own confrontations. But it was dreamy.

When he walked me home, I felt like I was sure. The way he acted at the party, the way he looked at me, I could just feel that he liked me. The certainty was amazing and a little scary. I felt almost comfortable, but I guess not quite. We stopped at the bike rack for his bike, and then we walked up to my apartment building's front door. That's when I jumped up on the front step because I was afraid that if I didn't, he'd try to kiss me. Or, worse, he'd think I was trying to get him to kiss me. I didn't think, I just jumped, but that must have been why. Honestly. It was like, halfway through being airborne, I could feel myself asking myself, "What the fuck?" My reflexes are assholes! But from the safety of six inches up, I told him I had fun and that we should hang out again. "Tomorrow?" he said. I must have said "Sure," and smiled, but I also think I floated off to a field of daisies and sunshine. I'd get a second chance to stand there. When I got upstairs I texted Rylee with an update, and she texted me back: "AHHHHHHH!!!!!!!!!!!!!!!!!!"

The next night he called me twice: once at five-thirty, to tell me that he'd call me at eight, and then again at eight. It was the cutest thing in the world, in the history of all world events. And I was calm, relatively. Even though it was the first time anything like this had ever happened, even if it had been (almost) twenty-four years waiting for something like this by then, even though I spent a lot of that time building these things up to be bigger and more terrifying than they'd really be, when really it would just look like walking somewhere next to someone and talking and doing my best—even still, I was, sort of, mostly calm. I guess I didn't know how worried I was that it (any of it, even these first-day things) would never happen for me until I was so relieved that it was. I could think someone liked me and be right. And it was someone I actually *knew*, and really liked, and had things in common with, and had talked to before. I felt like I could do it. Liking people you know—or getting to know the people you like, either order—is such a good idea. Fine, everyone was right.

From about six-thirty to eight I paced around my apartment, getting ready and talking to Rylee, who got back earlier than expected that afternoon. I straightened pieces of hair that were actually as straight as possible already. I reapplied mascara to a few choice eyelashes that just looked a little "off" to me. I took a Photo Booth picture of my outfit and emailed it to my friend Jenna for approval—she said, "Get it, girl!" and I was like "Yeeeeaaahh!!! But, oh my God, I am going to throw up." When he called, I asked if he wanted to come up to the apartment to meet Rylee's boyfriend, Andres, and so he did. Ideally, when I went downstairs to let him in, he would have told me I looked nice. But he didn't. It was a thought that I registered and then put neatly away, because it probably didn't matter or mean a thing. We went upstairs and sat in a little foursome and I don't have any idea what we talked about for twenty minutes because my ear canals were blocked by the sound of my brain working in overdrive. This was, after all, the first (or second? I STILL DON'T KNOW!) time I was going on anything even vaguely resembling a date. I didn't know what the fuck I was supposed to do.

Part of the reason I felt unprepared was that we were going

to an art show. I like art as much as the next person, in that I think colors are a good idea and I enjoy seeing them arranged in pleasing ways. When I studied abroad in Madrid and had basically no friends, I spent a lot of time wandering around the art museums and it was perfectly nice. Of course, that is probably because I was alone and didn't have to look or behave a certain way. I didn't need to act like the art was affecting me. I didn't need to say what I thought of any of it. With Spruce, I figured, I would need to like, interpret shit. Or comment on it. Or seem like I knew anything about it. And I don't.

After arriving and a brief, date-y misunderstanding about ticket payment (I was ahead of him in line so I paid for my ticket, walking in as he protested, saying, "Oh, I could've...I had it," me saying, "Oh it's fine!"), we were inside the art show. It was mostly just nice to walk around next to him, though I worried whenever too many moments passed without either of us saying anything. I just didn't have a lot to say, I guess. I was nervous; I can't say that enough. The local artists' work on display that night was good enough and some of it was great—there were some lovely paintings and beautiful prints, and a cartoonish drawing of happy little forest animals that I wish I owned.

But there was also a room full of garbage. We walked into the upstairs of the space (a building is called a space when it is filled with art, I learned) and into a dark little room, in which the corners were piled high with crumpled newspapers and plastic bottles. I'm serious! What do you do with that, when there are no brooms handy? "I like that little man," I said, pointing to a paper doll–type figure propped on top of one of the piles. I don't know. I was trying.

Somewhere between the room of twine (Me: "Is that glue?"

Him: "I think it's twine." Me: "That is going to be a real pain to clean up later." Him: "...") and floor lanterns and the post-art-show musical act that was slightly terrible, I lost my footing a little bit. It was going well, sort of—he offered to split a beer with me, and I figured that you don't just offer to share germs with someone you find disgusting. But it was hard to talk while the music was playing. He stood to my left, so I clamped my left hand around my right arm because I didn't want it just hanging there, at my side, like I wanted him to hold it. Even though I did. How do two people ever understand that they like each other enough that it's okay for one of them to hold the other one's hand? I don't get how anyone gets to the point where he or she feels comfortable taking that risk.

After a while Spruce asked if I was having a good time, which was awful. I felt bad, thinking that my anxiety might be show-ing up like disappointment on my face. I turned to him and smiled and said "Yes! I really am!" and I meant it. Because even though it wasn't great, it also still felt like it could be.

When the band stopped their set, Spruce asked if I was ready to go. He had a housewarming party to get to (to which he didn't invite me, but I figured it was small?), so he walked me back toward my apartment. Not all the way back, though. I registered that, too. He dropped me at the corner, told me it was nice to see me, and took off on his skateboard. I walked back upstairs and told Rylee everything. "I don't know," I said. "Nothing really happened and I feel like I was disappointing in my lack of art expertise." "No way," said Rylee. "Andres said you two are for sure going to date. I don't know how he knows that, but that's what he said." Having a boy confirm my hopes helped, because when you don't know anything about boys you tend to believe that one of them might as well be able to speak for all of them. And when I say "you," I mean me. You're probably better than that.

A week after that it was nothing again. I did the exact same thing I had done two weeks earlier: I consulted my cabinet. (I also sometimes call my friends my cabinet.) I took baths. I listened to sad music and changed my mind four hundred times a day as to whether or not I was wasting my time. It was one of those completely awful (but thrilling, exhausting, amazing) situations in which I had just enough reason to hold out hope, and those reasons, half the time, weighed fifty times the reasons I had to pack up and head for the boy equivalent of greener pastures. The other half of the time, I despaired. I wanted things to go differently this time, for once, for the first time ever. I just wasn't sure I believed they could.

All he did was confuse me. When we went to a Halloween party together, we giggled on the phone for fifteen minutes beforehand, and then when he came up to my apartment to get me, he didn't say anything about my costume. Even though it was adorable, even though I was a sparkly robot with a silver face. At the party he suggested that we dance, but then he kept abandoning me to run off and talk to his friends. He offered me some of his drink, but then jokingly asked if I was going to get my lipstick on him if I had some. What did that MEAN? Was that code for "Make out with me, please?" I have had it up to here (I'm holding my hand above my head) with boy codes. I don't like them. If I were brave or a different person, I would have kissed him and said, "I guess so," or something equally saucy. But I am me, so I gave him an "Are you serious?" bitch face: half joking, half not. Bri, in town for the weekend to visit, told Spruce's friend that she thought we'd make a cute couple, because she is an expert and she was fishing for information. He told her that he thought we were already dating. Who knows, maybe we were. I would not be surprised if other people could assess that sort of information about me better than I could.

At my birthday party two weeks later, it was the same, only more so. There were so many things that seemed like they meant something good, but I had to hedge them all. He brought me a present, but it was a brown bag with five of those little liquor bottles you can get on airplanes. He called me pretty, sort of, but only to explain why the bartender was nicer to me than to him. He gently pushed my hair out of my face, but only in the context of making sure I was holding my weight in the group effort to suck down a fishbowl full of liquor. On the walk back, I looped my arm through his, and he put his hand on my lower back. But maybe that was just because the sidewalks were icy. I cannot be sure.

A small and quiet part of me knew, the morning after my birthday party. My friends thought I was crazy, because it seemed like things had gone really well. I sort of agreed. But I also felt this deep uneasiness that led me to pull out my stack of personal reference guides and look up the year 2009: the journal I had when I was writing about Jim. Maybe the story arc written there could just as easily have been written about Spruce. There was a cute boy, and he flirted with me and even threw in a few grand-ish gestures to make me momentarily sure, and all my friends agreed. But then it sort of just trailed off. What difference did it make if, this time, it went a little farther? Not one thing was changing. It was still mostly nothing, wasn't it?

So that week I wallowed around and felt shitty, and that was comforting. And I tried to talk myself into giving up completely, ahead of time, to save myself from drawing it out like I always used to. I went to my parents' house for Thanksgiving break and I thought about it as much as I possibly could, like a chore. I called all of my friends again and I told them I was worried and all the reasons why. I was hoping they wouldn't agree with me that it was probably over. They didn't, not at all.

I went back to my apartment and, in spite of all my best tries, felt better. There was so much snow that year, and we bought a Christmas tree, and got ready for the holiday party we'd planned to have for the weekend after Thanksgiving break. And somehow all of that made me feel like it might still happen. He'd be at the party, after all. And you know what else? I was sick and fucking tired of having to prove to myself that somebody liked me. I was wearing myself out. I always used to let myself feel crazy. I always used to tell myself I made it all up anyway, that nothing I'd seen was legitimate and it was just so like me to get my hopes up over someone I barely knew. I used to tell myself I'd been acting like a stupid teenager. I was twenty-four now. I don't know if I was acting twenty-four, whatever that means, but I was acting like *one* twenty-four-year-old. I was doing the best I could with the information I had, and the information I had was that Spruce liked me, dammit. I was reasonable. I was right. I had to be, for once.

So he came over on the night of the party, the first one there. He was always early. We planned to have our guests help us decorate the tree after handmade ornament making, and while he made his, he made fun of my inability to construct a paper snowflake like the ones we all used to make in kindergarten. I asked what he wanted to drink and he smiled and said, "What you're having." I felt so much better.

There was this moment, though, when he and I were sitting at the table side by side, and laughing, and I looked across to the kitchen, behind him, where Rylee stood preparing drinks. The reason I saw her is that she was trying to get my attention and shaking her head no, making a face that said "I am sorry." Our telekinesis is good, but not quite that good. I said, "What?" She said, "Never mind." So I forgot it.

The party went on for three hours, and everyone made adorable ornaments, we played games, and we drank. People started to leave around midnight. Spruce was one of the last to go, but when he and everyone else were gone, Rylee told me right away.

"He's got a girlfriend," she said. "Or he's dating someone, anyway."

I guess that was what the head-shaking in the kitchen had been about. She had been trying to prepare me. She didn't want me to spend the next three hours swooning, but of course I did. I didn't know. I had decided to be hopeful. But I guess when I had gone downstairs to let in another round of guests, and it was just him and her alone in our apartment, he had said, apropos of nothing, "I've been hanging out with a girl." I wish I could have heard the way he said it. The way Rylee mimics it sounds hesitant and teasing at the same time. It's unnatural. It's not like this is something he would have normally talked about with her. They were friends, but mostly because of me. So Rylee said, "Oh, haha, cool," because she didn't care to hear that news and had no idea what else to say. And he said, "Yeah, definitely." So I'll never forget that he did it that way. On purpose, deliberately, really deliberately, when I wasn't there to hear it, but in a way he must have known would get that information relayed to me later on. Because he knew.

Rylee told me while we stood in our living room and I had her repeat the whole thing, twice. I was looking for contradictory evidence, but only because that was a habit. I knew, I knew. It was just so quick, that's all.

So I sat down on the couch—collapsed, really—and started crying and I did that for quite some time. I didn't say a thing.

And I wasn't just devastated. I was also pissed. I didn't even get a chance to fuck it up, or give up, on my own.

When my crying had slowed from deep-lung heaving to eye-watering, Rylee, in a touching effort to give me some tangible means of expressing my anger, handed me an incomplete tree ornament that a friend had made earlier in the night. It was this navy blue and orange monster thing made out of construction paper and glitter, with a word bubble hanging off the mouth that had been left empty. She asked me: "If there were one sentence that explained everything you feel right now, what would it be?" I thought about it for a second.

"I fucking hope that *everyone dies.*"

So Rylee wrote it down in the bubble, hung the monster on the tree, and sat down with me again. She rested her hand on my back until I stood up. And then we went to bed. I'd been talking about him for months. I couldn't think of anything else to say.

Tell Me If You Like Me

I STARTED MOURNING RIGHT AWAY. I was too tired to cry when I woke up, though I might've tried once or twice, just for something to do. I did not get dressed. I lay in bed until the need to fulfill basic human functions could not be put off any longer. I got mad at my lunch for making me need it. In the afternoon, for comfort, to kill even twenty minutes of my horrible day, I decided to watch my favorite episode of *Sex and the City*, which is "The Post-it Always Sticks Twice." It's the episode in the generally weird fifth season right after Berger breaks up with Carrie on a Post-it note. I felt that. I felt similarly betrayed by cowardice. It's one of the very few episodes in which I find Carrie Bradshaw truly relatable. She gets hurt and she turns comically angry, attention seeking, and dramatic. She yells at a stranger on the sidewalk. She decides to get dolled up and go out with her girlfriends, and then she runs off at the mouth when she sees Berger's friends at the bar. And then, because nothing else is helping, she decides to get high.

Attraction to stoner boys aside, my anti-drug stance had persisted pretty strongly. I don't especially know why. D.A.R.E. obviously had some kind of lingering impact on me, and then there is my involuntarily strict deference to the law. But that day, watching that episode with Rylee, I said to her, "That is what I need. Drugs." And, much to my surprise, she responded, "Oh, well I have some right here." Apparently, her then-boyfriend had asked to leave a little unopened vial of pot behind with her after visiting one weekend, because he was taking an airplane back home and couldn't fly with it. For five minutes I chastised her for temporarily allowing illicit substances in our home, sullying our apartment's good name. But then she said to me, "I think what we need to do, for you to feel better, is to get high and play Dream Phone." And there wasn't really much to think about, right then. I told her, "That is a really good idea."

————

I think I've probably had my copy of Milton Bradley's Dream Phone board game for about twelve years. The game came out in 1996, when I was ten years old. I think I got my copy two or three years after that, very nearly at the age when it was no longer okay to admit to playing it if you were trying to get any-where in seventh-grade society.

My copy of Dream Phone is now torn up from repeated use by my friends, my brothers, and me. I want to note that boys love that game. I think toy companies should know that. Nobody markets games like Dream Phone and Mall Madness to little boys, because everything that involves the color pink, love, home economics, or shopping has to be targeted to girls. But this is dumb for many reasons, one of which is that every American kid likes pretending to use a phone and every American kid likes pretending to use a credit card.

Though I love it very much, there are some seriously troubling undertones to the concept behind Dream Phone. Probably the most insidious problem, and the one that took me the longest to recognize, is that the entire premise of the game is a lie. Supposedly you, as a player, are trying to figure out which boy among a group of sixteen likes you. But since the boy only likes the game's winner, the game is *actually* about having a group of girls compete for the same dumb, indiscriminate boy. He doesn't like *you*, necessarily. He just likes whichever girl jumps through enough hoops and makes enough embarrassing phone calls to track him down and get ahold of him first. Even though, in that winning call, the boy will say, "You're right, I really like you!" he is really saying this: "There is nothing special about you, but you called me before anyone else could. Fair's fair."

There is also the problem of the interview process, which I find improbable, to say the least. I'm supposed to believe that one boy managed to gather fifteen of his close, personal friends into a mass participatory campaign to lead a girl (it doesn't matter who) to him through evasive interrogation procedures? And that each boy was assigned a particular clue and made to wait patiently by the home telephone until some girl called for it? And that the central boy himself would give a clue about himself, in the *third person*, unless directed with special instructions—the Star key—to reveal his feelings? This kid sounds like a maniac. I don't even think anyone should be that interested in him, to be honest.

What's worse still are the clues themselves. Why must they always be in the negative? In Dream Phone, the boys on the line like to pronounce their clue category at a normal volume, and then share the real secret in a whisper. "I know where he hangs out!...*It's not at the snack shop.*" Time and time again, these boys insist they *know* what your admirer eats, wears, plays, and does in his spare time. But they only ever seem to tell you what he *isn't* doing, which is a little condescending and also a waste of everyone's time. If Bruce had just told me that Scott liked hot dogs in the first place instead of being coy about it, I wouldn't have needed to bother Phil, or Dave, or Carlos. "He'll eat almost anything?" Not according to Phil ("EXCEPT candy!"), Dave ("EXCEPT popcorn!"), and Carlos ("EXCEPT pizza!"). Don't even get me started on the clothes. But fine, I'll talk about the clothes. It's nice to hear that Scott's friend Mike thinks he looks cool in whatever he wears. But it starts getting weird when Alan also says it. Jamal, too. They don't even change their wording a little bit. It seems like they might not genuinely think Scott dresses all that great. And why would he not wear blue jeans? Who doesn't wear blue jeans? Is Scott an old man? Gross. Scott seems gross.

The only realistic part of Dream Phone is that sometimes you call a real jackass who will yell, "I KNOW WHO IT IS, BUT I'M NOT TELLING! HA! HA!" Thank you, Spencer. I can see you still have some tiny shred of free will left. Your haircut leads me to believe you are navy bound. I think that's probably a good idea at this point. Just get out. Get out while you still can.

Anyway, I'd like to offer my suggestions for a new, more realistic version of Dream Phone. It's called just Phone. Here are some examples of the calls you might have as a player in Phone:

1. You call Bobby.

Bobby: "Hello?"
You: "Hey, it's me."

Bobby: "Uhhh...who?"

You: "You know, Katie. From school."

Bobby: "Where did you get my number?"

You: "Doesn't matter. Where does the boy who likes me hang out?"

Bobby: "Who?"

You: "Never mind. Forget I called."

2. You call Andrew.

Andrew: "Yeah?"

You: "Hey, it's Katie, do you know what my admirer likes to eat?"

Andrew: "What? I don't know who your admirer even is! Are you sure you have one?"

You: "It's a simple question, Andrew. Tell me. What my admirer. Likes. To eat."

Andrew: "Okay okay! Fine! I think he likes...cheeseburgers! I saw him eat a cheeseburger once!"

You: "Thank you. That wasn't so hard, was it? Good-bye."

Andrew tells his dad. His dad tells the principal. You are suspended.

3. You call Dan.

You: "Hello, is this Dan?"

Dan: "Yes. Hey, Katie."

You: "How did you know it was me?"

Dan: "The principal sent out that letter."

You: "Goddammit. Okay listen up, Danny, I don't have all day. DOES HE WEAR A TIE OR NOT?"

Dan: "I don't know! Maybe if he had like, a wedding or something?"

You: "You are useless. You will never succeed beyond the eighth grade."

4. You call Alex.

You: "Alex."

Alex: "Oh my God. Ahh...uhhh...what do you want?"

You: "Do you like me?"

Alex: "Please don't hurt me."

You: "It all adds up, Alex. You eat cheeseburgers. I saw you at the mall. You would wear a tie, if you had a formal event that required it. You love me."

Alex: "I don't even know you."

You: "You will."

At some age when I was too old to feel okay admitting to still loving Dream Phone but too young to realize that nobody would care, I drew all over the board. Specifically, I drew, in ink, unappealing facial and hair accessories over the moony faces of the age-inappropriate babes the game's players were meant to be chasing after. Dale is no longer twenty-eight and captain of the medical school football team. He is a punk beyond his prime, wearing a dog-collar necklace and improbable eyeliner. Phil is no longer eight and altar boy–esque. He is just blue—literally and, most likely, figuratively.

I really regret doing that to my poor copy. I can't think of another time in my personal history when I've deliberately defaced something of my own. It is among the most rebellious things I've ever done, which is sad if you're my friends and really great if you're my parents. They don't make this version of the game anymore—you can get a copy on eBay for twenty to forty dollars, but it wouldn't be the same. The modern version has unfortunately replaced the foot-long hot pink telephone with something closer to a cell phone. The new version doesn't even *have* boys' faces to color over when you're a teenager and disillusioned with life. It just has faceless masculine masses, which I have to admit sends today's young girls-who-like-boys its own important message: Some boy is going to break your heart. You'll call him up after interrogating dozens of his friends, and he'll say he likes you. But he'll be lying. And you'll never see it coming, because is a faceless, soulless, blob of a human being.

Still, Dream Phone and all its graffiti damage have stayed with me. It came with me to college. It came with me to grad school. I'm really good at it now because, technically speaking, I sometimes cheat. Don't read into the fact that I'm so desperate to have a fictional, scribbled-on mess of a young man tell me he likes me best that I would break the rules. I do need to hear, in his tinny electronic voice, "You're right! I *really* like you!" so badly that I am willing to sabotage my own human friends in order to win. But I don't think that has anything to do with anything.

———

Our late-afternoon, minimally drug-fueled game of Dream Phone started normally enough, though I did notice that I kept getting the same clue, round after round, despite calling different boys. "He's good at most sports...but not soccer." But not soccer. But not soccer. But not soccer. If my brain had been operating at full capacity, I might have thought to say something about it. But as it was, I wrote it off as a coincidence (?) and kept passing the phone back to Rylee when I was done with my calls. Perhaps this boy just really hated soccer.

She and I played Dream Phone for twenty minutes before I realized that she was accidentally restarting the game on every turn. The phone from the 1996 version has a little gray button below the numbered keypad that resets the game if pressed, and she was pressing it before every single phone call she made. I wasn't getting repeat clues because there was some glitch in the game. I was getting repeat clues because Rylee was a stoned idiot.

When we realized what had happened, the two of us laughed really hard, so hard we cried. And it was stupid and juvenile and, technically speaking, illegal, but I was, however briefly, happily distracted.

———

The worst thing—one of them, anyway—about someone who hurts you but is not visibly and outright nasty to you is that you have very little validation for wishing he'd be hit by a meteor, but you wish for that anyway. In the weeks after the Incident, I slandered Spruce's name (real and fake) up and down the apartment, but then also felt guilty about it from time to time, because for some reason my value system has to make me feel bad for wishing death upon others. For ten hours of the day I cycled back and forth between depression and anger, for ten minutes I bargained ("Maybe he just needed to date someone else for a little bit to realize that what he really wants is ME"), and for another few hours I passive-aggressively accepted what had happened. "Maybe he liked both of us and wasn't sure how to handle it," I told Rylee. "I'm sure he didn't mean to hurt me. It's just that he's such a fucking *asshole* that he couldn't help it."

There were times, in the immediate aftermath, when I thought that I was okay and had gotten over it surprisingly quickly. But then something would happen, and it usually had to do with seeing him, or, worse, seeing him and her together. There was another holiday party we'd agreed to go to long before all this, hosted by other friends from our school, and I guess the reason I still went is because I wanted to seem fine. But it was so soon. She came in the door before him, and we were standing right there in the entry, and I don't know how but I just knew it was her. She just looked exactly right—cool, well dressed, pretty. Beautiful, really. He introduced us all. He made me have to touch her.

At the end of the party he came up to Rylee and me and told us he was leaving, and I said "Uh, okay?" in this toxic voice, a cheerful outer layer with pure careless bitch wrapped up tight inside, like I couldn't possibly imagine why he would think we would care about his comings and goings. That is, at least, what I was going for. He was mostly already gone by the time I finished saying it.

So I went home and went to my bathroom and closed the door, and then I climbed into the sink. I sat on the counter, setting my feet and as much of my legs as I could fit inside the basin. I don't know why; it wasn't comfortable. It made sense at the time. I curled up and hugged my knees and cried, and the next time I sat up to check how sad I looked in the mirror, I saw that a long, dark streak of mascara had appeared across the outside of my wrist. This stunned me into silence for a moment. But then it sort of made me start crying again.

The next morning, Rylee made me a comic strip that featured me chainsawing Spruce's head off and then walking away in a leather jacket, smoking a cigarette. It helped.

I saw them together again just a week later, at yet another holiday party held by friends before the long winter break. I didn't want to go. Rylee was already home in Chicago, so she wouldn't be there to help me do a better job, knowing she'd be watching us interact, feeling that protective pressure to act like everything was okay. But I have to tell you this because I want you to be proud: I nailed it, I really did. I was funny that night, and I held people's attention, and I didn't shrink into my chair in anxious silence. I made party friends with her, even, the way people in food lines together do, joking about the cheeses or whatever. And we sat by each other. And I thought, if this person wasn't my predetermined enemy, I'd like her, I think. It sounds like we have similar interests. She is very nice. She laughs at my jokes. She is coming to get seconds with me. But I do wish she didn't have to look so pretty in her dress. I do wish my socks did not have holes in them. I do wish she wasn't her.

And I do wish that we didn't end up sitting in a line, me-her-Spruce, Spruce calling me charming with her there in the middle. It wasn't a big thing, it didn't matter and it wasn't weird of him, necessarily, to say something offhand about my school-related mass emails being charming, but it felt weird to have to be there and hear it, the way we were sitting. It was an overwrought artistic detail that I did not particularly care for.

But it was all okay, otherwise, and I went home feeling simultaneously very pleased with myself for not being a girl who hates other girls because of a guy, and convinced that I had done the best I could to prove to Spruce the error of his choices through my wit and my warmness toward the girl he was clearly going to have to break up with.

These are not compatible attitudes, in normal people.

But I wanted something else to think about, because the other thoughts that started to seep into my brain later that night and the next morning and for too long a time after that were the ones that sounded like these: He just didn't like you as much as he likes her, and now you know some of the reasons. She seems calmer, for one. Sophisticated. And looks aren't everything and you shouldn't even be thinking about this because there's nothing you can do about it if it's part of the reason, but she's prettier. She just is. It seems objectively clear. Black eyes, round lips, and big perfect teeth—features you've always liked and wanted from the faces of other girls. The way she dresses and does her hair makes you feel pretty sure that she would know what to say at an art show. That's superficial extrapolating, you guess, but sometimes you really can just tell, the way you knew it was her before you even met her. There would be a game show, match the boy with the appropriate girlfriend from this group of possible girlfriends, and you would put her next to him. You are stupid. You're not even in that group. You're off somewhere else, at home, maybe, looking up weird diseases and Bigfoot sightings on the Internet.

Here was the first time I ever felt bad about myself—not my flirting abilities, or my boy-related anxiety, or my unshakeable unintentional innocence about all of this bullshit, but *myself*, my personality and the things I do with my time and the way my face looks. Really. It just had never occurred to me to think that anything inherent to me was to blame for the things that went wrong (or the things that never even happened at all) with the other guys before him. Maybe it was all that time I'd had to decide I was cool and good and worthy without anyone else's help, I'm not sure. It wasn't a transition I noticed happening. It just was. It had simply always seemed clear there were other limiting factors more relevant than me the person, like previously existing girlfriends or insurmountable social-strata differences or the fact that we were twelve. I always liked me. And I didn't realize I'd never felt badly about myself until that was all I could do. So I'm mad that he fucked that strong streak up for me.

I saw him once over winter break. I was selling my old textbooks at the campus bookstore with a friend, dressed like total shit, and we came up the escalator to hear my name being yelled in our general direction. I looked up to see Spruce standing there with a duffel bag, headed out of town in a moment, and I thought, *WHAT is he doing here.* Then I said it out loud. I couldn't help it. "What are you DOING here?" I didn't mean here, the bookstore, really. I meant here, still on this planet. Why.

It didn't matter much that I'd come, over winter break and the next month after that especially, to realize that there were aspects of his personality that I would not enjoy in a romantic partnership—the propensity to prefer conversations about *things* and niche topics to conversations about people, for one, or the inability to sit still for more than three minutes at a time, for another. The fact that he wasn't crazy about me, too. That was probably one of the more major things. It didn't matter that

I didn't want to be with him, really. I still didn't want him to be with anyone else. Or happy, for that matter. I felt like burying himself alive was the least he could do to make amends for what he'd done to me—which was what, exactly? That was one of his other great and evil tricks: never saying or confirming a thing, never doing anything so outright vicious to the point that I, at least, could know that I had the right to feel terrible.

Instead I felt bad about feeling bad—one of the worst bads to feel—and limited myself to only the smallest and least noticeable acts of revenge. Early in the new semester, I had lent him some class notes (a brief "acceptance stage" moment of weakness) and I came to regret that simple kindness almost immediately. When I saw him a few days later, him greeting me happily in the hallway, I refused to look him in the eye. "Can I have my notes back, please," I said. He said sure and handed them back, and I snatched them, hesitating only to mutter "SEE YA" in a tone that I hoped conveyed everything I wanted it to: hostility, sadness, anger, strength, confidence, and maybe just a little bit of sexiness. I took off down the hallway without another look. It felt fairly monumental—I mean, I was so *rude*—but I guess he probably didn't even notice.

I daydreamed about confronting him someday, just to ask what happened and what he'd ever been thinking. Ideally I'd look amazing, like really, finally put-together this time, and he would look like he just got run over by a truck. I would ask him to explain himself, and he'd turn to me with a sad and weary look in his eyes and say, "I liked you very much. But I knew I could not make you happy, because you need someone who shines as brilliantly as you do." And I'd look demurely down at my feet and smile to myself, and then I'd punch him in the face, because that is some serious bullshit and I can't believe he would dare to try that in my daydreams, of all places. Of course I knew that if I were to talk to him about it in real life it would be a disaster, and that I'd probably end up more confused than I was when I started. Real life is just no place for emotionally honest confessionals between the sexes.

So I kept thinking that maybe I should have known—*really* known—earlier on. Maybe I should have given up before Halloween, or after the first time he started grilling me on my rapper preferences. Maybe I should have known right when I filed away those little complaints or signs of faltering interest, like the night he walked me only part of the way back. And not only that, not only was I to blame for not quitting sooner, but maybe it was also my fault for not trying harder for longer. Both these things, at the same time, were my problem. It doesn't matter if it doesn't make sense.

I kept seeing them and seeing them. Before all of this happened, he had been Rylee's and my main social life. He and his friends were the people we had hung out with on the weekends. So it seemed weird, or obvious, to suddenly cut that all off, to prevent ourselves from going to things we wanted to go to because of them, or to not invite them to things we planned when surely all of our mutual friends would notice and wonder why. And it got a little better all spring and I didn't mind it so much, but it was still awful when, in May, we invited him and her to our apartment for an end-of-the-year party, and I had to watch him put his arm around her shoulder. They were going to be together forever, weren't they? We only had a dozen or so people at that party. There was no way not to see it. I don't know what I was thinking.

But then school was over—me for the year, him for good. I wasn't going to have to see him anymore. I wasn't going to have to walk around school, all these vaguely tall and thin boy shapes making my heart shoot into my throat in fear until I got close enough to see that they didn't look like him at all. I wasn't going to have to walk anywhere where he might be at all anymore.

And it's not that seeing him after that or seeing him now would make me emotionally confused, or would make me think I still liked him or wished things would have worked out, or anything else like that. It's that I know I'd have to be nice, and I really hate having to be nice against my will. I would have to smile and ask how he was, because we'll always be people who used to like each other. Unless he really does get hit by a meteor. Then I will be someone who used to like him, and he will be someone with no memory, and his girlfriend will have to be the Channing Tatum to his Rachel McAdams in *The Vow*. They'll figure it out, and I'm sure they will still be very happy living on a deserted beachy island, somewhere where they have no connections to or ways to communicate with the outside world. And I could be satisfied knowing that my memory of us was the only true memory there was, even if only because it was the last one left. And it's not (necessarily) that I really want it to go down like that. But I made myself stop thinking about confronting him. I lost interest in hearing his side of the story.

My version should be the only version that counts. I was the one paying the most attention. I was the one who sat still through the whole thing. And if it wasn't a breakup because we weren't ever really anything, it was a heartbreak of some kind. It was different than all the rest because I say it was, I felt it was. It was really great and exciting and promising and then suddenly it was all wallowing and venom. I was standing on a table and he pulled the tablecloth out from under me, but he was a really shitty magician who never remembered any of the important details. And so I fell over, all the way to the ground. And I stayed down there for a long time, swearing. I was going to get up again, I knew that. It was just going to take longer this time.

Adventures in Online Dating:
Part One

TODAY IS MY TWENTY-FIFTH BIRTHDAY, which means that I successfully (?) got to the point I thought I would when I started writing this book. I am single, still, having always been, forever. Lest you think this was some sort of self-fulfilling prophecy, let me assure you: I didn't have to try at ALL. I made it twenty-five years without so much as a short-term boyfriend, quite easily. Congratulations! I did it.

I could tell you how I did it, but you know that by now, don't you? Lots of hopeful eye contact and then lots of running away. Lots of mild teasing. Many ill-advised pursuits. Too many pot-heads. And so on.

This time last year I thought this chapter in my life was nearly over, sort of. A week earlier I had spent my birthday party in an adorable outfit, making eyes with Spruce. The whole thing had seemed promising, relatively speaking. And then on my real birthday, though it was Thanksgiving that day, I waited around hoping he'd send me a text message or at least a Facebook post. Even though he'd told me happy birthday before, a few days earlier. Even though you can't really expect everyone to be attached to their phones on family holidays, even though my birthday often falls under the radar that way. Even though he was forgetful about pretty much everything, and I knew that.

That message never came. And when I think about the timing? That weekend is probably right about when he met the other girl, and the two of them started dating instead.

Here is a good tip I've learned: Don't like anybody who won't tell you happy birthday on your actual birthday. It will only be downhill from there. Someone who likes you, I think, will remember to take the time on the day you were born to say, "Hey, happy birthday," and in so doing, at least be willing to acknowledge that he is happier to have you alive than dead. Sure, you might be thinking, "Katie, just because someone forgets to tell you happy birthday doesn't mean they actively wish you were dead." And to that I guess I'd have to say, "Oh, sorry, I guess I didn't realize you were secretly surveying all of my so-called friends to see whether or not they'd mind if I fell off a cliff." And then I'd say I'm sorry, because this isn't about you.

I'd be lying if I said that some little part of me didn't think I'd have met my future spouse by now, and that we'd have been together for a year or maybe two. We would have already gone on a few vacations together—romantic ones, like Paris, or a cabin up north, or Harry Potter World or something. This is what happens when your parents married at the baby age of twenty-two and have been happily together for the twenty-seven years since. You start to think it always works out that way, or at least that it could. I mean, my dad always used to say that he saw my mom at the college cafeteria milk machine and knew then that she'd be his wife. The *milk machine*. How am I supposed to keep up with that?

I want to meet my true love that way. Not at a milk machine per se, because it would be kind of weird for that to happen now that I'm not spending any time in cafeterias, and I don't think I trust a man out of college who still drinks milk with every meal. I do, however, want to be seen from afar, and admired, and then wooed. By someone I adore right away. Basically, I want to expend minimal effort and have somebody fall madly in love with me just by virtue of being near me for a handful of days, and then it will just work out that we're perfect for one another. I do not see what the big deal is about that.

When I say things like this to my friends, they do these massive, comically exaggerated eye-rolls and tell me that it doesn't work that way, and that I'll never meet anybody just sitting around and waiting, and that if I'm such a feminist I should go make things happen for myself (like going out somewhere and yelling "I am a strong, self-possessed woman!! DATE ME!!" I guess), and that people don't meet each other like that these days. Yes, they sometimes meet in school. But mostly they meet at work, or they meet through friends. Or, worst of all, they meet online.

Now, I'm not knocking online dating in general (or if I am, it's only a little). I think it's a great tool for people whose life circumstances just don't afford them the opportunity to date very much or at all, or who just want another way to meet new people, and I know that many very happy couples meet in this way. I also know that almost everybody has got some level of hang-up about it and that nobody feels totally comfortable putting themselves out there on the Internet like that, and that there are tons and tons of normal, attractive, and great people with online dating profiles, and that the people I saw on there who looked like alien hybrids from *The X-Files* were the exceptions rather than the rule. I know that nobody should be embarrassed to try online dating. But I can't help it: I find the whole idea kind of mortifying.

My friend Marie, who approaches most areas of life with the kind of severe and exacting practicality that most people reserve for filing income taxes or applying for a mortgage, met her boyfriend of two years through OkCupid. She is incapable of letting her hormones and her neuroses drive her decisions, which makes her both helpful and extremely frustrating as a sidekick. She's also a few years older than me, so I like to pretend as though her wisdom and calm, focused demeanor are things I'll be able to attain after living a bit longer. For these reasons, I value her input, even when I hate it. And sometime last spring, when I was still mopey enough about Spruce to want to date *somebody* but before I was done feeling bitter about the entire world, Marie told me I should just try OkCupid already, and I grudgingly agreed.

It didn't go too well.

———

It was about 9:00 pm on a weeknight when I agreed to make my dating profile. I chose OkCupid because it was what my friends had used or were currently using, because it was free, and because it had the reputation of being the dating site of choice for urban twenty-somethings. Also, it had a nice blue background.

One of the things I hate about dating profiles is that it is nearly impossible to describe yourself without sounding either totally boring or completely insane. Very few people are able to sound like they're somewhere in between, even though most people surely are. I hate the broadness of a profile section called "A little about me." How is that possible? "I like happiness." "I am hungry a lot, and I like books." "One time I think I saw a UFO, but I was ten and it could have been anything and I don't want you to think that I'm crazy so I don't even know why I brought that up." The profiles I first examined (through the comfort and secrecy of Marie's profile) for "intel gathering," as I considered it, either left far too much to the imagination ("I'm a happy guy and if you want to know more about me, just ask.") or went all in to the point of recklessness. Describing ourselves, it turns out, is not something human beings are all that great at.

Still, I tried. With the assistance of Marie and Rylee, both of whom know how to make me sound better (or, at least, more approachable) than I do, I came up with something all right. I don't remember now what-all I said, but it's safe to say I made some stupid jokes, used too many exclamation points, and admitted too freely to my love of aliens. I activated the profile somewhere around 10:00 pm, and for the next hour the three of us sat on my couch and perused my options. We scrolled through twelve pages of matches, and I found just two of those people slightly appealing. I realize that might make me sound like an asshole, so let me clarify: It's not that I'm some hugely elitist looks-judge or that I had a field day criticizing everyone's music and movie tastes. I am no interests snob. I listed the Harry Potter books in order of how much I liked them in my "favorite books" section, for God's sake. Still, we can't help who we are and are not attracted to. Also, everyone was really short. I guess it's probably terrible as a five-foot-eleven-inch-tall lady to direct most of my attention toward people my height or even taller. At least, that's what my friends (five feet to five-six) tell me. Friends whose boyfriends, by the way, are universally six feet or taller.

I went to bed feeling dismissive of the whole thing, sure that I couldn't feel any worse about online dating than I did at that moment. When I woke up the next morning to see if anything transformational had happened overnight, I proved myself wrong. Overnight, I had acquired three messages. Two were variations on "Hey what's up." One of these came from the boringest person ever of all time. Another came from a young man whose interests included "guns—the bigger the better." The third message came from a twenty-one-year-old, whose existence outside the confines of my listed twenty-four-to-thirty-year-old age preference seemed not to bother him, and who told me, "Hey your really beautiful just so you know." I could have written back "YOU MEANT YOU'RE," but I guess it's best not to look a compliment horse in the grammar. Still, we were not meant to be. His picture was of him flexing in the mirror. We were a 47 percent match. But at least he complimented me. That was nice.

I took one last trip through my matches to see if anyone perfect had showed up in the wee hours of the morning, and I did find someone new—we were a 90 percent match, which is a pretty phenomenal score considering I answered the majority of my match questions with "I don't know," because I sort of find it hard to say what I will and will not tolerate in a mate in absolute terms (well, except for the obvious will-nots: Bestiality.

Adultery. Misogyny. Being a White Sox fan.). I clicked on his profile and found what must surely be the best/worst "about me" description given in the history of online dating. I won't quote the whole thing (though I definitely did so in an email to about seven of my friends) because I feel like that would probably be illegal and maybe a little mean spirited since he didn't ask me to read it. I will paraphrase, though, and say that he said that he lived the life of a broken music box from Thailand, made by "odious" and expensive child labor and mailed to America in "wasteful packaging." He said that the journey from Thailand made "his" music distorted, and that now he plays "eerie and irritating" tunes. He said that he sits (figuratively, I hope!) in a dusty garage, waiting until the day when he's sent to the garbage dump.

I mean, wow. What does that *mean*? I think he seems to be anti–child labor, maybe, so that's good. He also sounds a bit environmentally conscious, with the whole "wasteful packaging" thing, so that's good, too. But then there are the parts where he compares himself to a music box that is eerie and irritating. There was also a part about wanting to be like a donkey that I can't even really get into without dying. Soooo.

This is who Cupid *himself* considers to be my match made in heaven.

I shut down my profile after a mere twelve hours. I think it was too much all at once. I wasn't prepared for the guy who, in his "about me" section, described the entire scientific process of evolution and then ended it with "So here I am," NOT in a way intended to be humorous. I wasn't prepared for the overwhelming number of people who describe themselves as "living life one day at a time," as though there are tons of other ways to do it.

("Oh, me? I like to live my life *eight* days at a time. Really spices things up.")

Most of all, I wasn't prepared to put myself out there like that, because you know what I'm starting to think? I am just a big, huge, enormous scaredy-cat.

Adventures in Online Dating:
Part Two

Now I knew, very literally, that love wasn't going to happen overnight. I am obviously not a patient person. Nor am I very accepting of change. But after taking a little while—or, fine, like eight or ten months—to recover from my first horrible attempt at online dating, I also knew that if I really wanted to meet someone as much as I was saying I did, I might have to step outside my Comfort Zone, which is what I call my flannel pajamas, and into the big, hopeful, scary world of Internet dating. For real this time. Maybe I'd meet someone incredible on there, and it wouldn't unfold in the way that I'd been imagining it for twenty-five years, and that would be okay. We could have our own milk machine. Or maybe I wouldn't meet anyone. Maybe I'd meet several non-incredible people. There wouldn't be any way to find out if I didn't try.

So, I thought. So: Here goes nothing.

It didn't start out so badly. Jenna—who had agreed to having a go at round two right along with me—came over on a Wednesday night, because it was February first, and we decided that something like this should happen on a first day of the month. We poured ourselves glasses of wine and set about describing ourselves in the best, most attractive, most unique, most intriguing ways we possibly could. We were truthful, though. Mostly. I mean, yes, technically I'm five-eleven and a half, but I'm not going to round up to six feet online, am I? That's what I had listed on my previous profile (I felt it was best to begin this round with a clean slate) and look where that got me. Is this what guys are thinking when they list their heights as five-ten even though you know, in your heart, that they are five-seven? But in reverse? Goddammit. This is why online dating is terrible.

But that first night was fine. I had myself signed in to chat accidentally, because I didn't even realize it was there. When a little message popped up in the bottom right-hand corner of my screen saying "Hello, tall girl," I screamed. I checked out the profile of the guy who'd messaged me—tall, dorky, kind of funny—and though I didn't find him all that attractive, I impulsively decided to chat with him anyway. He was a boy who wanted to talk to me! On the first day of online dating, that is sort of all you really need. I honestly don't even know what we talked about. I think I was just overwhelmed by how much it took me back to middle school, flirting (well, talking) with boys on AIM for the first time. It didn't matter what he looked like (or what I look like, for that matter), or if we had anything in common, or what we were even talking about. He was a *boy*. Talking to *me*. On the INTERNET.

That small, youthful joy does not last very long.

Clearly I did something wrong with my profile the first time around to get only three messages in my twelve hours there, because in the same amount of time, with my new profile, I got twenty-one. "You sound less hostile in this version," said my friend Marie. She was probably right. The first time I hadn't wanted to be there at ALL. This time I was only mostly bitter about it. This time I didn't have a Star Wars reference in my user name. This time the "message me if…" section of my profile wasn't blisteringly, uninvitingly specific. It actually just said "…if you want to!" and, frankly, I'm starting to think that that might have been a bit *too* welcoming.

———

In a month on OkCupid, I received around 130 messages. I say "around" because I deleted so many of them immediately (having them sit in my inbox felt contaminating) that I cannot report with scientific precision the exact count. I don't think this number makes me special. I actually think it makes me decidedly *un*-special, because to many of the messages' authors I was clearly no more than one more female-looking thing who might be intrigued by the dashing brevity of a message reading only "sup?" Everyone was always telling me that, if nothing else, having an online dating profile would be a confidence booster because of all the flattering messages I'd receive.

This is abject bullshit.

Of the many, many things that my messages could have been called, "flattering" is not one of them. More fitting would be "trite," "absurd," "weirdly insulting," and "grotesque expressions of the soul-sucking vortex known as humanity." Some messages were innocuous enough, but these were in the minority. A few precious gems were legitimately nice and pleasant, but their presence in my inbox was so minuscule as to hardly be noticeable. If

I didn't have corrective contact lenses, I wouldn't have even been able to see them. (Or anything, really. But whatever, you get my point.) These messages were like these little lifesavers thrown out to me, a person who was drowning in a cesspool of filth and sewage water, only to be just as quickly cast aside because, even though they were nice enough, relatively speaking, the guys who sent them were fifty-two years old or were self-described "fitness models" or went by the user name "LetsFckAround."

Look, I know it isn't easy out there for dudes, either. (Isn't it? I think it actually could be. *Easier*, anyway. Less horrifying.) For some reason it seems like standard operating procedure, among those with opposite-sex interests, that GUYS message GIRLS and that is that. My understanding is that girls who message guys will be viewed by many of them as at least slightly unhinged. (A disclaimer: I've definitely heard this, but I've also been known to take too seriously any advice that lets me do as few scary things as possible.) I think this is on the way out, but it's lingering. It's just like the fucking Snowball all over again. So guys have some pressure—they're the ones who have to "make a move" and then just wait while my friends and I gasp and laugh and email each other the complete garbage they've just sent us. I would feel bad, except that the authors of the messages that provoke that kind of reaction most certainly do not give a fuck. You know how I know? Because they sent that same exact masturbatory-ass message to me AND two of my friends. Word. For. Word.

So I'm not sorry. I am, however, interested in the betterment of humankind. I am interested in historical records on some of the most pressing matters of our time. I am interested in the grouping and analysis of small disasters. So I've come up with a few categories of messages that you're liable to receive if you find yourself being simultaneously female and in possession of an online dating profile. May God have mercy on our souls, and may whoever invented the backhanded compliment as flirting tactic (damn you, popular MTV pickup artist Mystery!) be slowly roasted in a stew of his own fedoras, watched over by the legions of women who have to try to figure out why this person who ostensibly wants to date them just called them "pretty but not in an intimidating way."

Types of Messages You Will Receive during Your Time in Romantic Jail

1. The Neg

For the blissfully unacquainted, to "neg" someone is to basically insult her while pretending to compliment her. It's spitting in her face and then asking her out after. It is a statement that almost sounds nice if you aren't listening very closely. It's a thing you say to a woman if you are an asshole who believes that, ultimately, what women really want is for someone to be mean to them. Maybe there are some women who really like that! Far be it from me to deny a lady a good blow to her self-esteem now and again, if she promises me that's what she wants and she's really okay and she agrees to come hang out with me later, just girls. I just feel pretty safe saying that, as a whole, humans don't like when people are nasty to them. This is even true for women! I know, it's almost too crazy to believe.

Lo and behold, a few bravely delusional spirits soldier on.

Sometimes it's clear they know what they're doing, which is the worst possible type of neg. (The "know-neg"? I don't know.) Sometimes it's clear that they are just hapless goons. Sometimes it's just clear that you should have joined the convent like your third-grade teacher suggested. In any case, here are some all-too-real examples of negging in action.

a. "Oh man, my freshman year roommate was a total ISTJ, one of the worst guys I've known. However, I've since met some very nice ISTJs so I will give you a chance ;) Are you a standup comedian or do you like to make people laugh in a more natural setting? I actually have a room-mate who is/was a standup comedian but I've never heard him and don't find him particularly funny! Anyway, I hope I didn't insult you!"

Fine: This was before I realized that listing a Myers-Briggs personality type in a dating profile was gauche. I'm a sucker for quizzes and I was trying to save people time. But that's not the point! What this message really says is this: "Everyone I've ever met with characteristics similar to yours has repulsed me to my core. I do not enjoy other people, generally. Wink face. Sorry."

b. "What sort of writing do you prefer to do yourself? Do you have a three-ring binder filled with printed out pages of horrible poetry you've written over the years?"

This is such a *pure* neg. It's the outline of a polite question distilled by highly corrosive acid and then sprayed into my face with a high-powered hose. "Oh, you like writing? You're probably pretty bad at it, though, right? Wink face."

c. "haha sci-fi nerd?"

Okay, fine, this one is fair.

The list goes on. For the record, none of these messages garnered a response. None of these messages even garnered a half-second's *consideration* of a response. I know this was a surprise to many of these messages' authors, because I could see them returning to my profile for days afterward, checking to see if I'd been online. (If you haven't gotten the hint yet, online dating is creepy and terrifying.) Prior to OkC, I never got the feeling that anyone who was being mean to me was laboring under the impression that doing so would give me a sudden and inexplicable desire to drop my pants. Teasing, sure—where would *I* be without teasing as flirtation tactic?—but nothing on the level of the backhanded assholeish-ness that infiltrated my inbox from day one on OkCupid. I felt bad enough going online to date in the first place, but the influx of negs made me feel worse. It made me feel like I wasn't a person, and I guess to the people sending the messages, I wasn't. I was a profile. Maybe I'm being overly sensitive! But the desire to demean someone and the desire to date her are, I think, mutually exclusive. I could be wrong about that, though, because I'm just a woman.

Negging messages are probably the worst variety of online messages my friends and I received, but they are closely followed by another virulent strand—a sick infection kind of message, a message that starts off somewhere (maybe with a sick cow or chicken, one with access to the Internet) and spreads, rapidly, to

everyone. You don't know how it got loose in the human population and you don't really want to know. You just know it's
everywhere. It hits your friends first and that's when you know
you're a goner. You can try to escape, or believe that you are
different—immune, somehow—but you aren't. This sickness
does not discriminate, which is the main reason it is so dangerous. You'll know it by the feverish chills and the acute desire to
be euthanized in your sleep.

2. The Virus

On some level I was prepared for the assholes, because I know
enough people who've dated online, and have followed enough
blogs filled with online-dating horror stories, to know that good
manners and tenth-grade spelling abilities are underrepresented in
the world I'd so reluctantly just joined. What I was not prepared for
were the copy-pasters, the virus transmitters, the people who apparently send identical messages (or gently mutated versions thereof) to
the owner of every female profile they can find. I say "apparently"
because I wouldn't have known this was the case had I not signed
up for OkCupid along with Jenna, and later Rylee, and watched
with horror as our inboxes filled up with a not insubstantial number
of the very same messages from the very same users. I might have
noticed that there was something suspiciously hollow and generic
about these messages, but I would have allowed my belief in the
good of humanity to overrule the idea that anyone could be so gross
as to think that blanket dating messages could work.

I am often wrong about the good of humanity.

I realize that these young men probably don't consider the
fact that the women they're messaging might have persuaded a

few of their friends to suffer along with them, and that in doing so they will surely be comparing messages. I realize that some of them know this is the case and just don't care. I'll even concede that writing messages to prospective girlfriends/boyfriends can be an intimidating business, and that having an *outline* of a message that works well for one's personal style is not the gravest sin to ever be committed. But I am not talking about outlines or brief boilerplate messages. I am talking about missives. I am talking about excruciatingly detailed compliments. I am talking about sickness—a viral kind of pathology that sneaks up on you, tells you you're special, and then kills you.

Here are three perfect examples of the type of viral message I'm talking about, in increasing order of hysteria. They might look familiar. You've probably received them yourself.

> a. "Hi howz you doin!!!
> Just came across your post and really its seems to be very honest and clear
> I would surely like to know u better
> Well i am looking for a nice to be friends with and then take it from there
> and i really wanna take care of her
> I am pretty well off and well educated . . . and i guess i know how to treat a woman
> . . . coz i am a gentleman
> awaiting your reply. . . ."

We all got this message *at least* twice in our stays, of varying lengths, on OkCupid. This young man is overextending him-self. He's not just copy-pasting the same message to different people, he's copy-pasting it to the SAME people, multiple times. He's human spam.

b. "hi & how are you on this foggy minnesota night ? i must say that you seem like an intresting person from what i can tell from reading your profile and i would like to get to know you alittle better. i also must say that you have a stunning smile that would light up the darkest of nights & you look simply gorgeous in your pictures which i am sure do you no justice to how you look in person.

i hope that you had a wonderful wednesday & hey i look forward to hearing back from a beautiful lady such as yourself!"

Perhaps not surprisingly, this message came from someone with whom I shared a higher enemy percentage than match percentage. Ditto Jenna, ditto Rylee. He was like our *Sisterhood of the Traveling Pants*, but the opposite.

c. "I'm just being real here, I know this is completely random and I know you have entirely no clue who I am, but I was looking through profiles and saw yours and I was blown away. Like BOOM!!!! Absolutely blown away. You are beautiful. Not just the good looking girl you see occasionally, I'm talking like the kind of beauty that you don't EVER see. You know how a person addicted to drugs knows his drugs, he knows the "good shit" from the "not-so-good shit"? Well I know beauty. Its my drug. And you, are good shit! So I guess what I'm saying is…you are my drug…and I'm addicted. Haha. Your beauty is insane.

Like I said, I know this is random, but I had to let you know. I figured you probably hear it all the time, but hey, I couldn't let someone as gorgeous as you get away without me at least telling her first. Anyway, congratulations on being so magnificent. *applauds* Sorry if it annoyed you. If you want though, you should look at my profile, I worked really hard on it, haha, but there is a lot of information on there, so only go read it if you enjoy reading or you could hate your life. I tend to ramble."

When I first got this message, I had been on OkC for a few days and was already getting tired of the bullshit two-word messages and the negging and the total absence of shallow compliments I thought I'd be getting to at least compensate for the rest of the trash in my inbox. When this message came, and I was mildly flattered, it was only because my spirits were already broken. True, I still recognized it for the maniacal word vomit that it was, and true, I rolled my eyes so hard at "I know beauty. Its my drug" that my eyes fell out of my head and I had to pop them back in. But he called me "magnificent!" Such an underused compliment. I didn't respond, but I'm ashamed to admit that I kept that message because I thought it was really about me.

Then Jenna got the same message. Then Rylee got it, too. And then the three of us drove to West Virginia, where his profile said he lived (that's right, he's copy-pasting girls in *other states*), kidnapped him, carried him over our shoulders to a marble slab in a deserted forest clearing, and sacrificed his blood to the devil. He tried to cry out, but it was of no use. He tried to tell us that we really *were* all good shit, but it was too late.

3. *The Cry for Help*

There must come a time, after you've been online dating for months or even years, when you feel your spirit leaving your body. You'll stay online, but you won't even know why. You'll still sign in and look at people's profiles, just to pass the time, but you won't think of them as humans any longer. They might *look* like people, but then so do you, and you know that all you are anymore is a shell. You'll start flailing. It's hard to know for sure when it will happen, though my experience suggests that you're probably getting close when you find yourself sending messages like the ones below.

> a. "Aliens and UFOs huh. I saw one and when i messaged NASA about it they never even replied."

I know—this sounds like a joke. A funny one, even! You can't see his entire profile, but I could. It was definitely not a joke.

> b. "I need to laugh right now, since I was broken up with on Valentine's day. If you make me laugh it would be really cool. And we can discuss the annunaki, nibiru, and the blue spirals! That would make me happy. What would really make you happy?"

This was sent three days after Valentine's Day. :(

4. *It's Not You, It's Me. Me. ME.*

There are some people for whom sending that first OkCupid message is like being a guy bird puffing out his chest to impress girl birds. I don't know, I guess this works in nature. I'm pretty sure that if I were a girl bird, and I was minding my own business and regurgitating food to my kids from my first bird marriage or something, and some guy bird came up to me with his feathers all puffed out and his eyes bulging, I'd be like, "Are you seriously hitting on me while I'm throwing up?" But I guess I can't say for sure. Animal Planet seems to think this behavior has a pretty high success rate, and I think some of the males of our own species have taken note. Maybe because they can't make a first impression with clothing or intensely acidic cologne, some of the men on OkCupid peacock in a different way: bragging.

I like talking about myself as much as (and probably more than) the next person, OBVIOUSLY. It is my hope that by continually doing what I love to do, which is talking about myself, someone perfect will eventually just fall in love with me. So I understand the impulse to lead with yourself. But some part of me—the part that is familiar with social interactions and general guidelines of human conduct—recognizes that this is neither the most practical nor the most thoughtful way to get to know a person. Some part of me knows that what you are supposed to do when you want to get to know someone is ask him/her questions about him/herself, and not just because you hope you can then turn the conversation back around to you. Some part of me knows that I would never stroll into a bar announcing my various accomplishments and character traits to a guy I thought was hot—so why would I (or anyone in their right mind) do the same thing in a message?

It's that "right mind" part that really makes the difference, isn't it?

a. "well it looks like we could be friends…i think we should get to know each other. i am a kick ass son, brother, and friend but i would like you to find out for you self."

Aside from the fact that I can't imagine what one does to earn "kick ass" status as a son and a brother, this guy said he'd like for us to "get to know each other," but then went on to describe only himself. Then he challenged me to believe it. Does he even care if *I'm* a kick-ass daughter and sister??

b. "What a great smile! Any interest in a Triathlete ;-)"

It's like, you're so athletic that I almost didn't even notice you're forty-three!!!!

c. "Hello, so now I'm wondering how to entice a beautiful girl into responding to my email. Hmm, maybe bribe her with the option of cooking food for her, starting with something grilled or possibly stir fried. Then pull out the cheesecake I made a few hours prior along with some yummy fruit toppings. Mean while showing my humorous side in our delightful conversation on things we've done and hope to accomplish in our futures. Nah, maybe we just meet up and dive into a grand discussion walking around Mall of America, grab some coffee or tea and possibly take in some people watching or I carry the bags while you shop. Hmm, if she was up for adventure, we could go shoot some guns, indoor rock climbing, or snowboarding too. Guess I'll have to wait and see if she decides, here's an interesting guy that shows great promise."

I think he thinks this message is about me (or, rather, "she") because he's listing things he'd supposedly want to do with me, but it isn't. It's like some weird form of hypothetical showing off. I don't know that he can even do any of these things, nor does he have any reason to believe I'd have any interest in participating in these things. A brief glance at my profile would have revealed that I'm not the type of person who enjoys shooting guns, rock climbing, or generally any activities in which something going wrong means that I die. Plus, it mostly just sounds like he's going to try to make off with my mall purchases when I'm not looking.

    d. "NIce pic! care to chat sometime, maybe? I work in corporate IT management and Twincities being small for management consulting, I have to be little discreet about my fitness modeling! I have folks that work for/with me and they are used to seeing me in my meetings with tie and suit and dont want them to know about the fitness side and shirtless pics onine ahah"

THIS IS THE BEST. Not in a real way, obviously—not in a way where I'd ever want to respond, or meet him. It is the best in terms of the number of boasts it manages to fit in such a small message: 1) Has a "corporate" job; 2) Is a fitness model; 3) Has folks that work for him; 4) Owns suits and ties; 5) Looks good shirtless (presumably). Not to mention that he's only writing me to draw attention to his shirtless fitness-modeling pictures, to let me know that he doesn't want attention drawn to his shirtless fitness-modeling pictures.

e. "Are you one of those girls who won't date someone who's shorter than she is? If so i'll just stop right here."

Though this message is almost its own animal, a mixed-breed neg/cry for help/boast of sorts, I am categorizing it here because clearly this guy has been burned by tall girls before, and it couldn't have less to do with me if it tried. Why would I want to respond to someone who has already prepared himself to resent me and my snobby, exclusive height?

5. The Direct Offer of Sex/The Best Message I Ever Received

"UFOs Don't exist but my cock does and I'm home alone until tuesday do the arithmetic And no I'm not married"

What else can I really say? You get the idea, I get the idea, every one of us is in perfect agreement that this is the pinnacle of dating-message achievement and I got it all to myself. What's "the arithmetic," you ask? I don't know. It doesn't matter. You can't set this message up to questioning because opening that door will send you down an existentialist path from which you will never return. It's best to just enjoy it and move on.

6. The Mediocre

Finally, though I would be hard pressed to pinpoint and describe any of them among the mountains and mountains of filth I received while on OkC, there were some nice messages. Nothing spectacular, but how many spectacular first messages can there be in nature? I'm guessing that two total are sent per year, and though scientists try to encourage breeding, the messages are never really in the mood. And really, a first message doesn't NEED to be spectacular. If anyone is reading this and thinking that anything they send will be met with reflexive repulsion and a book chapter's worth of criticism, just know that the chances of that are, like, SO small. Literally write anything different from what you've just read and you will probably be okay.

For example, I got one very brief message that asked me to describe my Myers-Briggs personality type a bit more. It was kind of dumb, but so too was my decision to refer to my Myers-Briggs personality type in my dating profile (again, I'm SORRY! I was new!). When I clicked on the little face to the left of the message, I found a profile with a cute-looking blond boy, a few decent jokes, and an 89 percent match. So I did what I usually do when I find someone I think is cute with little to no supplementary information about his personality: I went crazy.

Buckets

IT TOOK HIM AWHILE TO TELL ME his real name, which was okay. Online dating gives you code names right off the bat, which is one thing about online dating I can support. In that respect, talking to my friends about how I didn't think the blond boy really liked me at all was the same as it had always been. Here's what that sounded like: "I just feel like if GarlicToast was interested in me, he would have replied to my last message by now." Rylee: "You are an idiot. It's been one day."

One of the things you're definitely not supposed to do when you like someone is try to match your personality to his or hers. It's quite hard to do this in real life anyway, at least for people who have a pretty clear sense of what we do and do not like to do. Like, I can pretend to know more about rap than I really do, but not for very long. I know this because I once told Spruce I thought that Drake, at times, sounded a lot like Lil Wayne, and he looked like he was going to cry. But on OkCupid, it is easy—dangerously so—to ape someone you find attractive. All you have to do is change your personality question responses to match theirs and watch your match percentage creep up point by point. It's thrilling.

It's a bad idea.

In those volatile first few days, when I hardly knew anything about who this Toast guy was, I pored over our respective personality questions. I looked for questions to which our answers were incompatible, and considered whether or not I *really* felt so strongly as my original answers indicated. Most of the time, I conveniently decided that no, I didn't. I didn't really HATE exercise. Maybe that was misleading. I could change it. I don't *mind* the elliptical. I always wish I were off of it when I am on it, but it's fine. With every answer that I revised, I boosted my match percentage with GarlicToast, because I kind of wanted us to be soul mates. After a few rounds of this self-editing matchmaking process, I would realize what I was doing and answer another ten new questions with my very honest reflexes. And then our match percentage would drop back down to where it started, and I'd go back to revising. Just a little. Just enough for a boost.

Our score wasn't low (it was a solid B-plus), and on the most important questions, our answers were compatible. It just didn't feel good enough. I guess since OkCupid was supposed to be my answer to a lifetime of being single—a lifetime spent creating false idols out of boys I hardly knew—I didn't want to accept that this, too, might not be it for me. I KNOW that is crazy. I know that I lost my head in an imperfect mathematical rubric for love. But Garlic (ugh), among all the creatures who had messaged me, was the only person on there who I was interested in who was also showing any interest in me. If it didn't work out on OkCupid—and if it didn't work out the first time, you can bet I'd be ready to call it off entirely—what would my next chance to meet someone be? How many years could I reasonably be expected to wait?

Being that I am me, all of this went down before I even knew his real name. Let's say that was "Neil." Neil and I exchanged twenty-six messages—about our jobs, our favorite TV shows, about nothing—before he asked me to meet him for drinks. After only a few hours of panic-wailing, I agreed. Though I am antsy and fearful in general, even I knew that I had no legitimate reason to turn down a date with someone who seemed cute, nice, and even a little funny. We settled on a hipster-y bar in Uptown Minneapolis, and I proposed the following Friday so that I'd have as much time as possible to drive myself insane with anxiety and self-doubt. We exchanged phone numbers, and all of a sudden I had checked off two very standard (but to me, monumental) Lifetime Achievements that I had been working for, on and off, for twenty-five years: I gave my phone number to a boy who I knew wanted it for romantic purposes, and I was going to go on a first date that I was SURE was a first date.

It was somehow both more exciting and less exciting than I expected. More exciting because I realized that this was something I could *do*, and I probably wasn't, as I had long expected, a mutant human destined to ward off potential suitors at the first sign of interest. Less exciting because I didn't feel like an especially changed woman, and also because I spent most of the week feeling like I was going to throw up.

I put a countdown on my whiteboard, the number of days until the date written in giant purple font, and "DAYS UNTIL DOOMSDAY" written underneath in black. I felt pretty okay at days five and four. I knew that a date was out there, in the future, but it was still far enough off to feel theoretical. Like anything you look forward to with some mix of excitement and dread, it still felt like something that would eventually become a memory without actually having to go through with it. Days three and two felt a little more desperate. I started worrying about how I'd be able to find parking. When I'm set to (reluctantly) participate in a social situation that makes me anxious, I direct that fear into the locale's parking setup. If there is a spacious parking lot specifically assigned to the place I'm going, I'm usually able to take comfort in that fact. If there isn't a parking lot and the place I'm going is in the middle of the city, I tend to back out if at all possible. I mean, who knows what could happen if I can't find a parking spot? I could get into a parallel-parking accident and find myself decapitated, and what use am I to anyone without a head? In the case of my date's destination, the bar had a parking lot—but only a small one—which I knew because I Google Mapped it ahead of time to make sure. I wrote down driving directions (the bar was fifteen minutes from my apartment, but it's good to be prepared) and felt momentarily better, until I realized I still had to decide what to wear.

Getting ready for a date isn't fun. It just isn't. I feel betrayed in this regard. I have watched a lot—a LOT—of romantic comedies that depict girls getting ready for first dates in high-strung frantic mode, accompanied by girl pop music and flattering lighting. They're usually stressed, but it's always in that clumsy-fun way that "awkward" girls in romantic comedies tend to be. She might have to bend over in a strange way to get her zipper to go all the way up. She might have one piece of hair turn out a little weird from the curling iron, and then give the mirror a hilarious look, like, "Why ME, why am I always such a total fuck-up? Ugh, MY HAIR!" She might be running late, hopping around the bathroom on one foot while pulling tights on over the other, and then she falls into the tub! This is how you know she's adorable and real, and that she's going to be in love within half an hour. By the time the guy picks her up (and he always picks her up), she looks perfect and composed, and she has a wonderful time.

I can hardly remember my date-prep process, because it was so unpleasant that my brain has tried to erase the memory of it from my mental filing system. I was meeting Neil at seven (obviously, one does not get picked up by an online date, who are all serial killers until proven innocent), so naturally I started getting ready around four. This was, after all, the first time I'd be meeting the person I'd come to think of as my likely soul mate—not because I knew all that much about him, not because our online conversations were charming and sexy, and certainly not because I'd ever been right about anything before in my life. It just seemed that, given the probability of my having gone as long as I had without finding *anyone*, a soul mate was OWED me. It didn't matter if I didn't even want to meet a prospective husband now, or get married in the next five years, or ten, or at all. It just sounded like the appropriate, storybook auto-complete to the start of my life. "Oh yeah, NO one thought she'd meet ANYone, and then she found true love with the first guy she ever dated!" And I'd shrug and smile graciously, like, "Haha, life," but it would be in this way that wouldn't annoy my friends or anyone single.

I mean, everyone always says you meet someone when you least expect it, and I never expected to find myself going on a date with someone I met online.

So I started getting ready at four. I wore an outfit that hit that perfect "slutty but also scholarly" note (tight top, wool pleated skirt, tights and boots) and got my hair to look reasonably non-terrible, which is the best I can ever hope for under high-pressure situations. I did my makeup and put on perfume. By then it was five-fifteen, and I had an hour and a half more before I had to leave. While I waited, I asked Rylee for advice.

"What am I going to talk to him about? I'm not good at thinking of interesting questions," I said, more shrill than I intended.

"Just ask him about himself," she said.

"What if he's really boring and I don't WANT to know more about him?" I asked.

"Then you can just say you have to head out. That is literally the worst-case scenario," she said, even though she must have known that was not true. The worst-case scenario was that I got murdered and cannibalized *at* the bar, in front of everyone.

"What do I do if he tries to kiss me at the end?" I asked, because as we all now know, I don't know what to do when confronted with the possibility of end-of-date kissing.

"He won't," she said. "If he is at all normal and nice, I really don't think he'll try to kiss you after having literally just met you, unless the date is SO incredible that you both know you want to kiss."

That made me feel better. I mean, I always want everyone to kiss me, but I also don't want anyone to ever even think about trying any funny business because I swear to God I will yell and run. It's sort of hard to explain.

When I left, Rylee told me to text her at some point to let her know I was still alive. She wished me luck and told me everything would be fine, and that at least, if nothing else, I'd be getting the fear of my first real official no-question-about-it date over with. As best friends often are, she was right. It was fine.

I got to the bar eight minutes late because I had a hard time finding parking—the appointed parking lot was full, and I had to circle the block to find an expensive garage. I considered this a harbinger of things to come. I walked into the bar to find it wall-to-wall with cool-looking people with tattoos and weird hair. I made my way to the back of the bar, and suddenly Neil was at a table right in front of me looking surprisingly like a real human being. He stood up and hugged me right away, which was a little odd, but friendly. He looked enough like his pictures in that it was fair of him to use the ones he'd chosen, but also different to the point that my doubts about online dating were reinforced. You just can't get the whole image of a person—their body size relative to yours, their skin up close, the way they speak and the mannerisms they use when they do so—from the Internet. I know this is why you're eventually supposed to meet your matches in real life, but I hate that online dating makes you start with incomplete data. (I say this as if I knew everything about all the other boys I've ever liked, but God, can't you just ever let anything go?) For instance, I couldn't tell ahead of time that Neil's shoulders would be about as narrow as my own—not a dealbreaker or anything, but just a surprise given my own relative narrowness. I couldn't tell what his laugh would sound like. I couldn't tell, from his profile, that he'd have an unnerving habit of raising one eyebrow while listening to me speak, as if every word I said were somewhat perplexing. (Note: This is not an impossibility.)

This is not to say that everything went poorly, because it

didn't. At least I don't think it did. I'm still trying to figure that out. I was there for five hours, and how many things can last five hours while being simultaneously terrible? (Monsoons. Hurricanes. Forest fires.) There were no awkward lulls like I had feared there would be. He didn't say anything insulting or rude. There were no giant, glaring red flags, like "At home, where my wife and three children live..." or "On the weekends I enjoy public nudity and shooting squirrels in the park." These are the sorts of things you prepare yourself for, to some degree, when you decide to pursue online dating, because these are the horror stories with which we have all become familiar. I had escape plans in mind in the event that something went terribly awry. What I wasn't ready for was a date that was so thoroughly and oppressively *fine*.

I mean, maybe "oppressively" is a bit harsh. It's not like I couldn't breathe, or was forbidden from using the bathroom or anything. It was just a little dull. My skirt was digging into my waist, too, which made laughing feel like a punishment. Luckily (?), I didn't have to do too much of it. Neil wasn't completely unfunny, but his jokes were so...*joke-y* that I felt more like the one-woman audience to a bad stand-up show than I did like someone on a date with a humorous person. Then there was his penchant for bringing up his glory high school days. He told me, a weirdly high number of times, about various high school teachers that had adored him, and why. It got to be so egregious that I said, only half jokingly, "I don't know why you keep telling me how much your teachers loved you." I don't know why I said it out loud. I think I was in shock. He just laughed.

Neil was also extraordinarily wholesome, to the point where he repeatedly used the phrase "what the buckets," or sometimes just "buckets!" Buckets, presumably, was a friendly and clean alternative to my beloved f-word. I've never heard that phrase or term before and I hope never to hear it again. I would not be surprised to learn that I visibly cringed on the third and fourth times he used the expression, once I had become certain that yes, really, that WAS what he was saying. Swearing too much is annoying, and swearing too little is not even a thing that can be done because nobody is bothered by the *absence* of swearing, but swearing in the form of folksy alternatives should be constitutionally prohibited. In the first few days after the date, when the word was reverberating around my eardrums while I tried to suppress the urge to let it bother me, I asked a couple of friends if *they* had heard the slang before. The looks of incredulity and sheer horror on their faces were unlike any I had seen in my time on this earth. They calmed me.

But Neil and I talked for five hours, and when I noticed that it had been that long, I told him I had better get home because I had a school-related interview to do early the next morning. I was exhausted—from talking so much, from scrutinizing, from the slow (and then, quick) realization that this person was probably not the soul mate I'd stupidly built him up to be after all. He paid for my drinks, because I couldn't quite figure out the correct amount of protesting I should do before giving up, and then we walked out together. He hugged me again outside the bar, but didn't say anything about seeing me again. I assumed he didn't feel it, either. I said "Thanks! Maybe talk to you later?" because I didn't know what else to say. As I walked to my car, I checked my phone and found five increasingly panicky text messages from Rylee, who had grown concerned that I was being kidnapped. She was apparently about to come look for me, but I texted a quick apology for not checking my phone on the sly earlier, and told her I was coming home, very much (mostly) alive.

When I got home, I found Rylee and our friend Silvana waiting for me in the living room. It was 12:45 am—*well* past Rylee's bedtime, and my own. I sat down with them for the post-game show, which is something we all knew would be happening without really needing to discuss it. If nothing else, this seemed like one good thing about dating: sitting down with your friends afterward to patiently and wisely dissect your evening. This is how we're all able to survive. I certainly didn't have the tools with which to understand what had happened, or whether I ever wanted to do it again, or why anyone even tries in the first place. I needed help.

Rylee and Silvana both asked, "Soooooo, how waaaassss iiiiit?" in that coy little voice girls use with each other whenever potential romance is involved.

"Ummmmmmm, it was fine!!" I said. That sounded weird, too enthusiastic.

"Like good fine?" asked Rylee.

"Errr, fine fine. I think I just sound excited because I'm so happy it's over with," I said.

"*Oh*," they said. "You were there for such a long time, though! What did you talk about??"

"I don't really remember," I said. It was true—both because I have a terrible memory, and because very little of what we had talked about had had any sort of impact on me. But then I remembered a few things.

"He told me several times about how much his high school teachers liked him," I said. "And he used the term 'buckets' as a stand-in for 'fuck.'"

A few moments of silence followed. These things take processing.

"Was he nice, though? Was he cute?" asked Silvana.

"Yeah. I mean…yeah. Nice, definitely. Cute, sort of? Like sometimes I would find myself looking at him and being like, 'Yeah, he IS cute!' and then other times I would be like 'I don't know why his face has to get like that when he laughs,'" I said.

"I think that if you had a fine time, and he was nice enough and cute enough, you should go on a second date with him. If he asks. Because sometimes it takes two dates to really know," said Silvana. Silvana is married and though she is young, I tend to think of her as someone who doesn't know what it's like out there. She's always thinking everyone deserves all these chances and that you shouldn't go around judging people by their covers, which is ridiculous.

"Ummm, maybe!" I said. "He didn't say anything about hanging out again so maybe it won't come up. I don't really want to have to make that decision."

"At least you did it," said Rylee. "Now you know that you can go on more first dates and live to tell the tale."

"No," I said. "I am never doing that AGAIN." I was only partly kidding.

———

Neil did ask me out on a second date, something I hadn't entirely been expecting given the lack of mention of it at the end of our first date. He texted me a few times, first just to chat about a TV show we'd talked about, and then to ask if I wanted to see a comedy show that week. When that last text came in, I called an emergency cabinet meeting. Or, rather, several sequential cabinet phone calls, as my friends don't have the decency to fly in from all parts of the country whenever I have a pressing question about boys. Rylee leads and closes cabinet consultations, so after I got her advice (somewhat surprisingly, given her insidery information about me and my success in this field, she erred on the side of not going if I felt there was no chemistry at our first date), I called Colleen and Bri. I texted Jenna. I went downstairs to ask Marie and Silvana. In between each call or visit I'd report back to Rylee, just to make sure all opinions were granted her second opinion. Colleen, predictably, agreed with whatever sentence I had presented most recently. (Me: "I don't want to go." Colleen: "Yeah, I don't think you have to. Sometimes you just don't feel it!" Me: "But what if it takes longer for feelings to develop?" Colleen: "Yeah, true, you know, maybe it's best to give it another chance.") Bri said I should go, and so did Marie and Silvana. Jenna told me I should do whatever I felt comfortable with—typical, supportive bullshit that doesn't give me what I really want: someone to make my decisions for me.

The thing that really confused me was the way my frequently coupled girlfriends took the date's fineness as an indicator that I should give it another try. If it wasn't outright unpleasant, they said, then why not see him again?

One of the great divides, I think, between people who date a lot and people who date never is that people who date never don't understand putting up with "fine." I can't begin to conceive of why anybody would voluntarily spend great chunks of her free time dedicated to someone she doesn't adore, because I never do that. My dater friends, on the other hand, do this *all the time*. I know this because I'm the one they meet up with after, and I'm the one who has to try to understand why my otherwise brilliant friends keep hanging out with people about whom they only have bad (or very, very mediocre) things to say. A person who has spent her life planning her free time based only on herself, and the friends she knows she loves, can't understand this. Why would I want to go out to dinner and a movie with someone I'm not completely crazy about when I already know how much I like eating dinner and watching a movie by myself, or with Rylee? Getting someone else involved means I have to put on a nicer outfit and stress out about the way I look chewing my food. If I'm going to have to consider my chewing face, I only want to do it for someone I think I might be able to really like. I know that might make it harder for me. I know there is a possibility—a very little one, though, that I have a hard time really believing in—that chemistry can grow where there wasn't any to begin with. I know that if I don't put myself out there, I won't just answer my door someday to find my perfect spouse waiting on the other side of the stoop. AND I know that if that did happen, I should probably call the police.

I always think about my collective cabinet as perfect, unbiased individuals who must inherently know more about my crushes and my flirtation techniques (that term being used loosely) and what I should do to make love happen for me more than I do, because they have been through all this—or things *like* this—before. I don't always listen to them, but when I don't listen, it has always made me feel like I'm doing something wrong—like I'm willfully going against the specific, time-tested directions of my wiser compatriots because I'm scared and stupid and naive. Thinking about *not* going on a second date with Neil, against the majority opinion of the cabinet, was making me feel overwhelmingly guilty, because who was I to think I knew anything about anything? My friends were acting like they knew the answer, probably because I was asking them to tell me the answer. My cabinet sometimes pushes me because they want me to be happy, and to some extent that happiness is presumed to come from being somebody's girlfriend. Sometimes I might need to be pushed. But sometimes I have to separate myself from my phone and stand still and be myself. Sometimes I have to trust that being me is also an okay path to take.

Besides, Rylee was on my side. She's a big proponent of instant chemistry or none at all. She also knows me better than the rest of the cabinet, so her vote has a proportionately higher weight than the rest. She made me feel like it was okay to turn down this latest opportunity to end my singlehood record—like there are things *I* can know, on my own, without having any field experience to back it up, just because I'm trustworthy, too. I am, after all, the president in this metaphor. The people wouldn't have elected me if they didn't think I knew how to make the right decisions.

So I texted Neil back to say that I couldn't make it, because I was too busy that week. That's the one thing I feel bad about—I should have been direct. Rylee told me that, early on, it might be better to just send a signal without saying "I'm not interested" explicitly, because that might just embarrass him. She might be right. I'm not sure. I'm starting to think that there isn't even such a thing as being "right" in, like, ANY of this relationship stuff. In any case, he didn't respond, and that was that.

I stayed on OkCupid for a couple of weeks after that, but my heart wasn't in it anymore. Or, rather, it was less in it than it was before. My heart was hanging over the edge of the OkCupid window, with just one little ventricle still grasping the ledge. (Gross.) It eventually got to the point where I was really only using the site to respond to sci-fi nerds to talk to them about UFOs.

It all became very exhausting. I wasn't interested in anyone who messaged me, and I felt more and more that there wasn't anything distinguishing me from the other girls these people were messaging. They just wanted *someone*. I know it can't always be like that, but in those last two weeks, it sure felt like it. And I didn't like that at all. I couldn't relate to that. I guess I came to realize that I didn't just want "someone." I didn't want to put that much of my energy into looking anymore. If a boyfriend was the prize I could get by putting myself up for display like that, wading through insane numbers of horrible, stupid, and sometimes offensive messages in the hopes that I'd find a few nice ones, going on endless fine first dates with people I hadn't seen in real life beforehand, and then going on more dates with people I wasn't drawn to because I had to learn patience, then online dating wasn't a game I was interested in playing. At least not right then. So I deleted my account.

Someday maybe I'll feel differently. Someday I might get bored of myself and find that I'm in a dating mood that isn't satisfied by the people I meet in my real life. Someday I might start feeling more ready for a lifelong partner, and I'll want to spread around my opportunities for meeting that person. Then, maybe, I'll go back online. But I'm just not sure I see it happening with OkCupid. To me, OkCupid is like the free zoo. There are some cute animals there that you can look at without paying a dime, but spending too much time there is just going to make you feel sad. The animal kingdom representation is always a little off—there are a couple really cool animals (your polar bears, your tigers), but there are way more flamingoes than you'd ever be interested in seeing. I'm fine with seeing a nice flamingo now and again—they're *fine*—but it's just not something I ever find myself missing when I'm happy and by myself.

Happily Ever After

WHEN I FIRST STARTED THIS BOOK, I assumed it would end with a wedding.

Not mine, obviously—that would be ludicrous—but Rylee's. She was dating a man named Andres whom she had met while working as a seasonal grounds-crew member at an arboretum. Andres was a full-time horticulturist and, naturally, he had a crush on Rylee from the day she started. She had another boyfriend when he first met her, but they broke up. Three weeks later—it wasn't a particularly tragic recovery period—she started dating Andres. A few weeks after that, something very, very strange happened. I realized that I thought he sounded great. Perfect, even. For basically the first time in my entire life, I thought I might actually like one of my friend's boyfriends.

It was something about the way she talked about him. There wasn't any hedging, no habits he had that she would complain about and subsequently defend when I asked her if she didn't think they might be a problem for her. She talked about him leaving M&M's and a can of Diet Coke (her two favorite food items) in her work cubby to surprise her. She talked about the two of them spending time running around outdoors, making each other laugh so hard they could hardly concentrate on Mario Kart, and having really good sex. She told me her family loved him, and that his loved her. It all kind of made me want to throw up, and I told her so. In a loving way. She knows me well enough to know that, from me, that was distinctively high praise.

I guess it was about three or four months in when I decided he was "the one." I don't mean "decided" in that I was going to arrange their marriage, but just that I felt very certain that they were going to be in love forever. I remember when I knew: We were on the phone, and she was telling me that, the past Friday, they had gone out drinking with work friends and on the walk home, they had taken turns pretending to throw up off the sidewalk, made sick by how much they physically repulsed one another. You know: like twenty-four-year-old girls and twenty-six-year-old boys do when they *really* like each other. It was the kind of thing that, before, only Rylee would have found hilarious. It was the kind of thing that other boyfriends ignored or nervously laughed at, or it was the kind of thing Rylee would have previously kept herself from doing in order to make herself more "suitable" to the person she was dating. So that was when I started a Word document for her wedding toast. I like to be prepared. Every time I opened it and tried to write a few words, I started crying. It was the first time I have ever cried from being happy. That's another reason I knew.

Rylee always wanted to find him so badly. She's talked about (or at least thought about) marriage with every boyfriend she's ever had. Even Aaron, the PowerPoint Presenter. Even the red-head hipster she dated for one month after she transferred, and even (improbably) the pothead Phish-loving hippie she dated for three weeks the year after that. Even everyone in between. These discussions (when relayed to me later) inspired varying levels of panic in me, depending on the particular boyfriend's relative awfulness. When Rylee started telling me she and Andres had started talking about getting married someday, I didn't worry. The thought had already occurred to me. Knowing that I thought they were meant to be made me feel better—because if someone was going to take my best friend away from me, he had better be goddamn flawless—and apparently Rylee knowing that *I* thought they were meant to be made *her* feel better, more sure that it was right. When she told me that, I happiness-cried again. "I told you that all those years of telling you I hated your other boyfriends would pay off," I told her. She just glared, but I knew it was in a way that meant, "You're right, and it is clear to me now that your unflinching rigidity and hostility toward my past boyfriends has been for my own good." It felt so good, the two of us agreeing on how great her boyfriend was for once. We could *both* be right.

And then we were wrong. Then, almost two years into their relationship, when she and I were both twenty-five, Andres cheated on Rylee. He drunkenly made out with the girl Rylee had always worried about—the one lingering fear she'd had about him, that he'd end up thinking of that girl as more than a friend—and then spent the rest of the night cuddling with her in her bed. It was winter break and Rylee was in Chicago, home from school. Andres told her what happened right before Christmas, though it had happened a week earlier. He had planned to wait until after Christmas, so she could "enjoy the holiday," but somehow Rylee got a feeling. She asked him on December twenty-third if he had ever cheated on her, and he said no. She asked him again—asked him to *swear*—and, that time, he said yes. She called me crying, right after he told her, from her car on the street outside his apartment. She was trying to run but couldn't quite get herself to do it. Under any other circumstances, I would have told her to leave and not look back. But we were adults now, and I was in shock. I could not believe this was happening. I wanted to kill him. But when she told me she thought she should go back inside and talk to him before making any rash decisions, I said I thought that was a good idea.

Before it actually happened, I think both Rylee and I believed that she wouldn't survive breaking up with Andres. I didn't know what she would do, but I had thought it would be reckless. She has spent her whole life looking for her husband, and I didn't know how she'd be able to live through losing the person she had decided was him. It's not that I didn't think she was strong. I did, and I do. But Rylee is impulsive and heartfelt and persistent, jumping into things before she's sure she's ready and often unwilling to break away unless she's forced. So I expected her to stay and try and work until he made her leave. And she did, for one week. But it wasn't him who made her go—he was the catalyst, but he was also too weak (a "fucking coward," in my preferred refrain) to tell her he wanted things to end. He would have passively gone along with whatever she decided, at least for a while. And she realized that. So Rylee did the bravest thing I've ever known her to do, and she left. She drove back to Minnesota a week before the end of winter break, because the man from whom she had been expecting an engagement ring had cheated on her at Christmastime. She didn't do anything crazy. She just cried—the whole drive home, and for the entire two weeks after that. It was more crying than I knew was possible, but it wasn't hysterical. It was the calmest round-the-clock sobbing a person could do.

The first few days gave me a false impression of her recovery rate, because she was too deep in shock to let any kind of finality sink in. She laughed at a few things here and there, and I thought that meant she'd be happy soon. You always forget that it's impossible to grieve every minute of the day. You always forget that a mourning period can include laughter, but just because it's there, it won't mean that you're really okay. It got worse before it got better. There were the aftermath phone calls with Andres, in which they both danced around the idea of leaving a renewed relationship a future option, and the talks we had afterward in which we both tried to decide whether holding out hope was a very good idea. I said I didn't think it was. She said she didn't even know how to rule out that chance, and wasn't sure she wanted to try.

Sometimes I heard her crying from my room. I'd go to check on her and she'd be in her (empty) bathtub. There is just something about bathroom basins that call out to a person who is crying about a guy. It's not comfortable and that's welcome because you don't want to BE comfortable. The porcelain and Formica are cold and unforgiving, just like SOME people you know.

The main thing she kept asking me was, "When am I going to feel better?" I told her, "Soon." Or I told her, "I don't know when, but you will." Or I told her, "It's just going to take time." These are the things we tell each other more because we want them to be true than because we know they will be. I mean, it's not like I could really be *sure* that her heart wouldn't get so heavy that it would slide out of place and into her feet, so that her heart rate would always have to be measured by a nurse holding her foot. I wasn't *certain* that Andres wouldn't mail her a package of the things she'd left behind, with a note reading "I always hated you AND, even though I can't see you, I think your hair looks dumb today." I wasn't sure that the world wouldn't one day soon fall off its axis and we'd all go sliding off the ends of the earth into space and suffocate. I'm still a little worried about that one, actually. But I wasn't going to tell her that. I was going to tell her that I *knew*, without a doubt, that everything was going to be okay. Just because I needed it to be.

I had always wanted there to be a reason for her to stay in Minneapolis forever, and not go back to Chicago as she had planned. I had always wanted us to live together and be single at the same time for any real length of time, just for once in our lives. We had gotten into little fights about this. I'd get upset when she'd delay something we planned to do because she had to talk to Andres on the phone, and I would tell her that I wished he wouldn't have to figure into every last thing we did. And because I don't know how to not say things that come into my mind, I would tell her that I just wished she was single sometimes. It was selfish in the way we sometimes want our most adored others to be ours alone. Her whole life has been spent looking for that in a man, and mine has been spent looking for it in a best friend who doesn't ever date anyone either and can be with me twenty-four hours a day—or at least some slightly tempered, less creepy-sounding version of the same. Now it looked like I would be getting what I wanted, but not in a way I would have ever wished for. She would stay because here at least she had a roommate and more job prospects. It was practical, and it was anticlimactic, because it didn't feel like something I should express excitement about. "Your boyfriend cheated on you and you have no future left in Chicago and so now you're staying with meeeee! YAYYYY!!!!" That would have been kind of rude.

Soon, though, there were signs that things really *were* going to get better. One day, about a month and a half after the breakup, when she was walking to class and I was back in the apartment, she texted me, "Even if I'm not totally over the Andres situation, I'm really happy I'm staying in Minnesota." I read that message, and then I involuntarily squealed, and then I locked it so I could keep it for as long as I have this phone, because I wanted tangible proof of the first time she'd ever said something loving about Minnesota to me. There was also the grief progress chart I'd drawn on her whiteboard after an especially long crying session of hers. It was a loop pattern that mimicked what I'd heard or read somewhere about progress looking like a spiral more often than a straight upward-sloping line. (I looked it up just now and it might have originated with a potty-training book? Seems appropriate.) There would be times when she started to feel better, but these would be followed by little periods of feeling worse. The thing to remember, I said, was that the periods of feeling worse would still be higher up than previous periods of feeling better. At the bottoms of the spirals Rylee drew cartoons of herself filling up various bodies of water with tears—bathtubs, pools, oceans. Sometime in late March, I walked into her room with her and noticed that the chart was gone. In its place were written her assignments and daily schedules on the board, just like she always used to do. Just like normal.

I kept waiting for the anger stage of the grief cycle—my favorite part of my friends' breakups, when we can be hyperbolically angry and shout-y together, a team of two against everyone who has ever wronged us—but it never came. She never said that she hated him, or that she wished his extremities would all fall off, or that he'd get caught in quicksand but that what would kill him would be the swarm of flesh-eating insects that attacked his head. And a few months later, when he came back around (like they always do, with her), asking if she thought they could ever get back together, and she said no, she just felt sorry. There wasn't any glory in it. There wasn't any reason to want revenge, or to hold that over him, because she didn't need it. There wasn't any fury to feed, no anger stage to get through on the way to acceptance. There weren't going to be any vindictive stick-figure comic strips made about him, or any tearing up of things he'd given to her, nights spent slandering his character. It wasn't that kind of breakup. We are getting older (and, allegedly, wiser), so maybe the relationships and the recovery aren't always so clear-cut. Sometimes you just love someone for as long as you can, up until it makes less sense for you to keep trying than it does for you to stop. You lose each other, and that is the end. There isn't really anything funny about it.

A couple of weeks ago I asked Rylee what the turning point was—the thing that made her know that she could get past this and not only live but maybe do better than she was doing before—and she said it was when she realized that she could do whatever she wanted, work wherever she wanted, and live wherever she wanted. She could live in Minnesota because it was best for her career and her happiness and because she wanted to be near her friends (Me! She meant me!). She didn't have to think about anyone else's goals or desires and then try to make them work with her own, or sacrifice opportunities she wanted because there was a future family to consider. It's not that she *wouldn't* do those things. It's just that she didn't HAVE to. She could live for herself and herself alone, and if what she wanted to do happened to match up with what someone she cared about wanted to do (like, say, me), then that was just great. When she was saying all this everything went sort of slow-motion for me, or maybe I was just only partially listening to have an inward epiphany at the same time (I would apologize to her, but she does this to me ALL THE TIME). I was somehow only then understanding that this freedom Rylee was describing was totally new to her. To me it sounded normal—a description of what it feels like to be not only single, but (relatively) unconcernedly so. This is the same freedom I've always had, for my whole entire life.

Epilogue
25 Years of Solitude

JUST LIKE MOST GIRLS, I have spent the majority of my growing-up years, on and off, in (sometimes intensive, usually half-assed, often theoretical) pursuit of cute boys. That's not to say that most of my time IN those years was spent on them—it wasn't, not by a long shot. But for most of my years, there has been at least one boy I was thinking about and hoping to date, in the abstract. In my chronology from birth to present, there has been a specific theoretical boyfriend in mind more often than there hasn't been. There aren't many ages you could name without me being able to think of the boy I liked that year. In fact, twenty-five might be my first. I am, however, only about halfway in. There is still time for me to ruin my year on someone with a questionable haircut or moral code. Plus, I've discovered what it's like to fall in love with people on Twitter. You don't even need code names when they don't live in your state. Sometimes I make them up anyway, to be safe.

My approach to dating (if you can fairly call it that) looked a lot like that of my peers for a long time, but at some point when we were growing up, everyone else found the easier, less rocky path up the mountain and forgot to tell me about it.

(Or was it on purpose??) Somewhere around the time we all became legal adults, everyone else really ramped up their skills, efforts, and successes, whereas I pretty much flatlined. I saw a few boulders in my way and was like, "Well, guess I'll just sit down here forever." There must be differences between the way a fourteen-year-old acts toward a boy she likes versus the way a twenty-five-year-old does, but I am still struggling to understand what they are supposed to be. Part of this is because I remain as clueless as I ever was, as ungifted at flirtation and seduction as always, as completely and irreversibly a Bermuda Triangle as the day I was born. But the other part of it is that I am just myself, all the time.

This is not to say that girls who date easily and often are not themselves—many of them are, because some people are just irresistible like that, and I hate them, but also love them—but rather that, for better and for worse, I have never learned to adapt my behavior and my presence to become any more appealing to the opposite sex than it is in its natural state. You can't tell me that's not a learned behavior for every non-Aphrodite among us. It totally is, and I know it, because while all of you have sat in bars chatting up the cute (and non-cute) guys who park themselves next to your stools, I have sat behind you, watching. I know, it's really scary! But that's the price you pay for being friends with a very tall, protective, no-nonsense, borderline-hostile person like me. I can get the creepy ones off your back in two seconds or less if you need my help, but I will also spy on you to try to understand your alien behavior. What I've started to understand is that the rest of you smile around strangers a lot more easily than I do, which I hear is good for your mood and which I *know* is good for making people fall in love with you.

You also tend to be patient (at least for a little while), kind, and receptive—even with the guys you have no romantic interest in. You are used to this. You put people in a holding pattern before you decide whether you want to allow them to board or destroy them with lasers. My decisions in that metaphor are much more impulsive and dangerous, and there is usually a lot more enemy fire. I yell "ABANDON SHIP" a lot, too, but that's mostly for theatrical purposes.

You are, unquestionably, better at this than I am.

I've just never been very good at strategizing. Rylee is, as you might expect, incredible at it. Playing Scrabble or dominoes with her is an absolute fucking nightmare. Watching TV shows or movies that SHOULD be suspenseful with her is a pain in the ass, because she almost always figures out what's going to happen and tells me about it halfway through. And when she finds a guy she wants to date, she outlines a plan of action (in her head; she's not a lunatic), follows it, and then *actually dates him*. There hasn't been a guy yet she's wanted to date whom she hasn't managed to at LEAST ferociously make out with. She is the Babe Ruth of daters.

This hasn't always been a positive thing for her. She's dated guys longer than she should have, made it hurt more than it needed to. She's dated guys who were unforgivably asshole-ish and awful. She has dated hippies and potheads, guys who don't shower and guys who don't put on real pants to leave the house, guys with secret high school girlfriends and guys who broke her heart. She might choose to change a few details here and there, if she could—for example, I think she'd have kept that PowerPoint presentation, for rainy days—but I don't think she'd take any of it back. Her experiences with those guys made her learn things about herself that made her ready to date someone better than the rest, like Andres. And then, when better than the rest turned out not to be good enough, they made her understand how to lose people and still have hope afterward. They helped teach her to be how she is today, which is happy.

My own history, while at the opposite end of the romantically active spectrum, is similarly uneven. I didn't date the varsity triathlete. I didn't ask the most popular kid in the sixth grade to roller-skate, even after he suggested that I could. I didn't protest when Dylan Campbell left me at midnight on a Saturday night to go do homework. I didn't say yes when my best guy friend asked me out when we were nineteen, and I didn't say yes when a similar thing happened with a different good friend six years later. I didn't tell Spruce directly how I felt about him, and I literally jumped away when I thought there was a small chance he might try to kiss me. I didn't say yes when Neil asked me out on a second date. I didn't try very hard to have bad dating adventures of my own. But I wouldn't change a single one of those events or choices if I had the chance. My experiences (or, ugh, lack thereof) made me good at being single. They made me sure of who I am and what I want (and don't want) in other people. They made me braver (very slowly and over time), and they made me look for confidence elsewhere. They gave me an extraordinary amount of free time with which to be around for my best friends' bad dating adventures instead. It's never occurred to me to put myself or my friends second to a boyfriend, because I've never had the option. After twenty-five years, I'm pretty sure that if I had it, I wouldn't take it. For that, I am happy.

―――――――

Of course, it's always a good idea to challenge yourself, and to learn to do something you could never have done before. That's why Rylee gives me lighthouse tips now and again, and that's why I'm trying to show her how to emit silent, stony hostility when she wants guys to leave her alone. I'd like to learn how to beckon a few good sailors in once in a while, and she wants to learn how to turn the light off for one second in her goddamn life. Well, I'm not sure she *wants* to, but she knows it would be a good idea to at least know how. Neither of us are quite sure how to teach each other things that come so naturally to us, but we have countless years ahead of us to work on it. For the first time in approximately ever, we are both single without (viable) prospects. It's almost like we're on an even playing field, except for the fact that her abilities and her pheromones put her dozens of yards closer to the end zone than I am. For instance: Once word spread around school (presumably through the Rylee-centric underground railroad all guys seem to use) that Rylee was single, she had no fewer than four gentleman callers texting her and emailing her, flirting with her and inviting her to their parties on the weekends. The lighthouse has been fully reactivated. It is hysterical to watch, and only partly annoying.

This time, though, she's going to be more selective. She's already turned a few boats away! And, now that she's sticking around, I'll be whirpooling myself closer to her, hoping to trick a few of those lost souls into my own depths. Or the equivalent of that, in a less creepy and sexual-sounding (but still somewhat sexual) way. Learning to not sound so scary is one of my other main goals.

So here we are. You've been listening to me this whole time, and are almost certainly completely intoxicated. You're sleeping over! Don't even try to tell me you're going home at this hour, because I won't hear it. Don't go to sleep yet! Don't even let your eyes close the tiniest bit or I swear to God I will get out the toothpicks.

The not-sounding-scary thing is just going to take a little time.

Every year that comes after this one is going to be one more opportunity for me to feel weird about being that age without having ever dated a soul. I can't promise you that won't ever hit me again. (Maybe you aren't asking me to promise. Maybe you're like, "Uh, you SHOULD feel weird." Why would you say something like that to me?) I am in a small minority that gets smaller with every minute, and sometimes that makes me feel very alone. Not even as much because of the being single part, but because there are fewer and fewer of my girlfriends with whom I can identify in that super-specific way all the time. It's basically just me now. Sometimes I count Colleen, but it's not really a fair call, because she did date that one guy for about six weeks a couple of years ago. They only saw each other like four times during that period, but still. And when she broke up with him she asked me to tell her what to say, and she wrote it down on note cards for when she called him, but STILL. She still doesn't really count.

And it's not just that I'm not doing things everyone else— or almost everyone else—is doing. I'm apparently not thinking about them, either. One day Rylee and I were at a museum, and after briefly talking to a guy who worked there, while we were walking away, she told me, "He was trying to flirt with you."

And I said, "Oh," because I hadn't realized it, because I almost never think that's happening unless it's really egregious. She was like, "Just 'oh'?" So I said, "Ummm, yeah?" And then she got a little mad at me. So we walked around the museum kind of arguing about guys, and that's how it eventually came out that Rylee evaluates whether each and every guy (every! one!) she meets and talks to might be into her. Not because she wants all of them to be into her, or thinks they all could be. It's just her first instinct to wonder. Hearing that made me stop in the middle of the hallway. I said, "I have literally never done that, with anyone. That has never occurred to me even once." And then SHE stopped in the middle of the hallway, and we just stared at each other for a long time, obstructing traffic, because neither of us could even begin to understand what the other was talking about. What's worse is that I went home and text-polled all of my girlfriends, and every single one of them said she did what Rylee does, at least most of the time. What the hell? This was, like, last week. Why didn't anyone tell me? Who ARE you people?

So it happens more often as I get older that I realize I live in a girl bubble of my own making. (Guys pass by on the outside, like ghost shadows, and sometimes I see a really hot one, but I avoid going out there if at all possible.) And I really do love it in here. It's insular and comfortable and all of the people I love best are inside, and there are days, especially whenever I find new girls that I love and bring them in here with us—non-creepily—I'm so happy I can't imagine feeling like there's something else I'm supposed to be looking for. I worry that you won't believe me, but maybe that's only because someone's been telling me single girls are trying and failing to be happy and I listened too closely even though I said I wasn't hearing it. (Single Girls: What Will We DO about Them?)

Here I have to fight the urge to get up on a soapbox and yell—I'm imagining me sneering the way Beyoncé does, looking killer in sunglasses like Hillary Clinton—and say that I don't need or even want some MAN because I am a FEMINIST, god-dammit, and that traditional romance is a tool of the patriarchy, and it's only women who are told (and who tell each other) that everyone deserves a chance, and that it's not my job to be a welcoming mat for dudes I don't even know, and that the pressure to make guys everything is intentional and is placed on girls so that we have less attention left to pay to everything else, and I want a crown that says Queen Bitch on it, and that I would love it if every girlfriend broke up with her boyfriend and joined the rest of us in an army whose job is to have a massive, girls-only, Robyn-soundtracked dance party for peace until, somehow—I haven't worked out the details—global warming is reversed and poverty eradicated. Also everyone's clothes look just perfect.

And I think some of that righteousness is reasonable, even if it started spiraling out of control toward the end. But it all exists within the same person who cries, without fail, at "Tale As Old As Time" in *Beauty & the Beast*. And at the old married couples in *When Harry Met Sally*. And when Seth tells Summer, "It's always been you," and then, a few episodes later, when he gets on that kissing booth and makes her stand up there with him, even though she's super popular and he is a nerd. And really I cry (or almost cry, or at least *feel* like crying) anytime two characters I like kiss each other and at least one of them is surprised it's actually happening, like they were waiting for this for a very long time. I cry at all of it. Only I pretend I'm not moved, and I point at whatever it is on the screen and say, "That's stupid." But I'm lying. I think it's really nice. I want that (or as close as real life can get me), and my soapbox, too.

I just don't have even one goddamn idea how to get there.

But whatever happens next, I made it this far. It wasn't bad at all. Only a few sink-crying episodes. The natural experiment—research question: Can anyone live for a quarter of a century while (partially) unintentionally single?—is over. I am being released from the lab, and my guess is that things will proceed roughly the same as before. Nobody else really knows that this was for science except me. But I think it's going to be fun. I think I'm going to embarrass myself again. I think I'm going to call my friends for advice more often than I should, but it's just because I love them so much and I want to talk to them every minute. And they really are so perfect and mean so much that it's hard to imagine I could meet anyone else who would make me as happy, much less even happier still.

But I think I will.

And that's not for any solid, logical reason. It's certainly not because my track record would indicate that it's only a matter of time, or because I've recently learned any secret seduction tricks I've been keeping hidden from you until this very moment. (How much would you throw up if the last thing I said here were something like, "Oh, just point your toes inward and blink and touch your womb area a lot," and then I flew out of here on a magic carpet with a boyfriend?)

I believe it's true because I've been thinking about it, and I just don't think there is any good reason for me not to. I mean, yes, you and I both know there were some very weird decisions made on my part, but still, I had my reasons, sort of. They made sense at the time, kind of. So if, and when, I do fall in love, I won't be all that surprised if I do so in spite of all my best—and bewildering—efforts to the contrary. Anyway, I have a lot of time. I have three whole quarter-centuries left to go before I'd even tie the previously held record in years of solitude. And when it happens, it's probably not going to look like anything I've watched on a screen. I'm finally accepting that, and I am—for the most part—excited about it. Falling in love is totally unimaginable to me. I think maybe the best things often are.

Acknowledgments

I used to have a few very vague ideas about wanting to someday write a book, but I'm doubtful I would have done anything about them had it not been for Allison Hunter, my wonderfully supportive, sharp, and extremely driven agent, who told me I should write a book and then, amazingly, read it when I did. I am so grateful to her (and everyone else at InkWell Management) for her input, for believing in me, and for encouraging me to shape my scattered list of stories into an actual book.

I want to thank the amazing Sara Weiss, my incredibly brilliant and talented editor, for having the nerve to recognize the exact parts of my earliest drafts in which my joking was self-defensive and telling me, as nicely as humanly possible, to cut the bullshit and be truthful, even when it was seriously really embarrassing. This book is a thousand times better because of her. Thanks, also, to everyone at Grand Central Publishing, for giving my book such a terrific home.

Thanks to Kate Lee, an early reader and a wise one. I am so appreciative of her support and insight.

Thanks to the enviably funny and wickedly smart Edith Zimmerman, for being the first stranger to read something I'd written and for telling me to do it again. Wanting to impress her has made me better. Without her early support—and her friendship—I don't think any of this would have happened. Thanks also to Jane Marie, Nicole Cliffe, and the readers of the Hairpin. You are all the best.

Thank you to Olivia Wilde, who once tweeted a link to one of my "Reading Between the Texts" pieces and, subsequently, made me scream in the office where I had a very boring internship that summer.

I want to thank the many friends who contributed to my life (and, therefore, this book) in their own ways, especially: Emily Basten, Silvana Hackett, Tara Hottman, Julie Kobs, Marie Kurth, Ian Mobley, Joke Raelateju, and Chris Stedman. Thanks to Chiara Atik for her advice, her patience, and her dedication to Gchat. Thank you to Emily Rhude, for growing up with me. Thanks to Briana Piché for her infectious enthusiasm, and to Joyce Jhang, my darling friend and best-ever bunk bed companion, for possessing the kind of loud, crazy laugh I want to make happen as much as possible.

I'm endlessly grateful to my lovely, frantic best friend Colleen McShane, for relating to me, for handling guys only just a little better than I can, and for the absolutely maniacal way she tells stories. I'm crazy about her.

And of course, with everything I have, I want to thank my best friend and soul mate, Rylee Main, the lighthouse, for being the kind of friend I was looking for over my first eighteen years, but somehow even better. I also want to thank Rylee for her (occasionally excruciating) memory for details: On some weekend soon after I started the book, when I already thought I was stuck, she took out her whiteboard and her markers and helped me outline every last crush from start to finish. When she and I talk about the book, she sometimes calls it "ours." She's right.

Finally, most importantly, I want to thank my family: my little brothers, Joe and Dan, the two best young men I know, and my parents, Paul and Dianne. For raising me, for loving me, and for never, even once, asking me when I'm going to get a boyfriend: Thank you.

About the Author

KATIE HEANEY is a writer and blogger whose writing has appeared on BuzzFeed, Outside magazine online, *New York* magazine's culture blog Vulture, The Hairpin, The Awl, and Glamour.com, among other places. You can find her on Twitter at @KTHeaney. She lives in Minneapolis with her best friend and a fish and, she thinks, a ghost.